CW00516763

FERRETING

FERRETING
An Essential Guide

Simon Whitehead

To Mikey
all the best and
Good luck in all your
~ferreting~ adventures.

Simon Whitehead

THE CROWOOD PRESS

First published in 2008 by
The Crowood Press Ltd
Ramsbury, Marlborough
Wiltshire SN8 2HR

www.crowood.com

British Library Cataloguing-in-Publication Data
A catalogue record for this book is available from the British
Library.

ISBN 978 1 84797 036 7

Disclaimer
The author and the publisher do not accept any responsibility or
liability of any kind in any manner whatsoever for any error or
omission, or any loss, damage, injury or adverse outcome incurred
as a result of the use of any of the information contained in this
book, or reliance upon it.

Frontispiece picture courtesy Steven Taylor.

Typeset by Magenta Publishing Ltd (www.magentapublishing.com)

Printed and bound in Singapore by Craft International Ltd

Contents

Dedication

This book is dedicated to all those who wish to promote the craft of the ferreter and to educate others in the skills involved in this traditional country pursuit.

Acknowledgements

The writing of this book has at times been a roller coaster of emotions, but I hope that the end result will be of interest to all those who ferret or enjoy country pursuits. I could not have compiled the book without the help, encouragement and assistance of so many friends. In particular, I would like to thank Steve Taylor for his countless hours, if not days, accompanying me around the countryside, experiencing his own journey with the camera; I hope his journey with the ferrets is as fruitful. His advice and excellent photographs are a testament to his passion for the countryside and the portrayal of its traditions. Also, thanks to Greg Knight, Craig McCann, Nigel Housden, Ivan Ambrose, Eaglemoss Publications Ltd and Bob Lee for their permission to use their photographs and illustration; Deben Group Industries for their help and support of the ferreting community; Bob, Kev, Torchie, Bill, John, Martin and Pat from Bridport Nets for their help, guidance and constructive comments relating to the netting section; and Ivan, Norman, Paul and Steve for their excellent help and much needed assistance over the years, long may it continue. And last, but definitely not least, my grateful thanks go to Jules, and our daughter, Grace. Jules has patiently tolerated my unusual lifestyle and provided me with unwavering support and encouragement.

The author and publishers are grateful to the following for the supply of photographs: Ivan Ambrose, Eaglemoss Publications Ltd/ The Hayward Art Group, Nigel Housden/ Pinsharp Photography, Greg Knight (www. ruralshots.com), Bob Lee, Craig McCann and Steven Taylor.

CHAPTER ONE

Acquiring and Caring for a Ferret

In the popular mind, ferreting has always been associated with the working class, being viewed as a rural pursuit that provided a chance for the workers to escape the harsh reality of their daily lives and sample the tranquillity and clean air of the countryside. In fact, workers engaged in ferreting out of necessity, in order to provide food for the table, although after long hours spent down the mines or in factories, the feeling of freedom they must have experienced once out ferreting is one that we cannot truly appreciate nowadays. However, contemporary ferreting still provides a way for people who are urban-based, due to work or family commitments, to sample what this green and glorious land has to offer whilst exercising the instinct we were born with, which is to hunt, whatever the quarry. In the following pages, we will consider in depth the art of working ferrets to catch rabbits.

Once the leaves start to fall, nature is warning us that the colder months are on the horizon and, with them, the ferreting season. To go ferreting, you will need some equipment and permission to hunt on private land, but, above all else, you will need a team of ferrets. Preparation for the new season should start just as the last one finishes, although unfortunately a large proportion of ferreters unwisely switch off from rabbit control come the end of the season. Some sell their ferrets, being unwilling to look after them during the vacant summer months, then restock the following autumn. These so-called ferreters are not worthy of the name; they are just people who go ferreting. Once the season has finished, just like a football team manager in the close season, a true ferreter's thoughts will turn towards the team of ferrets required for the forthcoming season. Decisions have to be made. Am I happy with my team as it is? Should I breed from my existing stock or bring in new blood? Where should I strengthen the team or do I need to replace any old stock?

For my own ferreting, I require many ferrets, from the fast, flowing ferret to the slow, methodical worker that is stubborn enough to stay and grind the rabbit down. All these types have a place, as the warrens worked over the year will be as individual as the ferrets themselves. In direct comparison with modern-day football, ferreting is now a squad game.

Ferrets are the most underestimated of our working animals. Over the years, the price of dogs has gone through the roof, while the price of a ferret has unfortunately remained low, with the result that people may purchase them without due consideration for their subsequent welfare. Also, we shouldn't forget that the ferret is a household pet across the nation. Since becoming a popular pet, their instinct to hunt has inadvertently been weakened. However, husbandry and sensible management of our ferrets should ensure that they reach the high standards we require. Only then will we be doing these little grafters the justice they truly deserve.

If you are a first-time ferreter, then you should set about learning as much as possible about ferret husbandry and management.

The apprenticeship of ferreting is a long and sometimes arduous journey. (Steven Taylor)

Much advice will be given within these pages, but there are also many good books on the market that deal specifically with this subject. If you are an old hand, it doesn't hurt to run through the basics once again. Getting the ferrets' welfare right will go a long way towards ensuring that they will work efficiently in the field. It should always be borne in mind that, as with all of our domesticated animals, we are responsible for our ferrets' welfare 365 days a year, through holidays in all weather conditions.

The manner in which our ferrets are kept is often dictated by our personal circumstances. The space available, the amount of ferrets kept and how often they are worked will suggest the best way to house them, although the basics remain the same despite differing circumstances. Ferrets require good housing and food, as well as plenty of handling, and it goes without saying that the more ferrets you have, the more time it will take to look after them. The average lifespan of the ferret is six years, although many now live longer than this. A working ferret's age might be lower, especially if it is worked a fair amount, but with higher welfare standards this age is slowly rising.

Try to ensure that you start off with good stock from a trustworthy breeder. The sale of ferrets at markets and shows is sadly rising and while the demand for the ferret is there, people will continue to breed ferret after ferret whatever stock is available, purely for financial gain. If a ferret costs only a few pounds, is its value being truly appreciated? The question we should be asking ourselves if we decide to buy a ferret from one of these venues is: Will they be up to the task we require of them?

THE FERRET

But first, let us explore the make-up of the ferret itself. The ferret is a combination of a well-proportioned, elongated body, lean, muscular legs, feet with pads under them and sharp claws. The claws are vital to the ferret, as they need these for hunting, climbing and clawing at their food. Their everyday lives include a lot of climbing and exploration of their housing in order to keep them mentally and physically stimulated whilst not out hunting. The ferret's head is streamlined, with a nose and whiskers that are designed to detect their quarry in the darkness of the underground hunting domain. Their eyesight isn't the best because they are working a lot underground. The body and functions of the ferret have been designed and evolved to suit their surroundings.

OPPOSITE: Another rabbit, another learning experience. (Greg Knight)

The ferret has an insatiable lust for hunting. (Greg Knight)

Ferret Colours

The colour of the ferret ranges from the popular albino, a white or creamy animal with red eyes, to the black polecat ferret, which bears the closest resemblance to the wild polecat. There are over twenty different colours and combinations, but as far as working is concerned it is just a matter of dark or light, white or coloured – colour doesn't distinguish between a good or bad working ferret.

The colour of a ferret doesn't affect its ability to work underground as it is in darkness. The rabbit cares little for colour in its bid to survive its encounter with a ferret, but colour does affect the way in which we perceive how the ferret works above ground. As our climate is changing, so are the animals and plants that live on and underneath its surface. The undergrowth is no longer dying back or hedgerows lying bare and the trees losing their leaves in the early seasonal months of September and October, with the result that there is a lot of greenery around at any given time of year. As our surroundings change, so must we. I now work a lot of white or lightly coloured ferrets as opposed to the darker ones, due to the ease of detection once back on top of the ground.

Many falsely believe that a true ferret is white and the darker polecat ferret is in fact a wild animal. The polecat is a wild animal; its name is simply used to describe the colouration of the wild ancestor on the domestic version. When I first started ferreting, only a

10

handful of colours was available but that was many moons ago and things have certainly changed since then. However, to say that one colour of ferret works better than another due to colour leading to specific personality traits is simply inaccurate.

THE JILL VERSUS THE HOB

The female ferret (known as the jill, bitch or doe) and the male ferret (known as the buck, hob, dog or jack) differ in many ways. The difference is not only physical in terms of size, shape and appearance, but also in their attitude to work as they can be affected by

hormones when coming into and during their breeding seasons. In the present climate, we have ferrets of all shapes and sizes, from minute ferrets of both sexes to ridiculously large ferrets. Both extremes, I find, are unsuitable for ferreting. Among normal-sized ferrets, the jill is the smaller of the sexes, usually by about a third, but she is powerfully proportioned with a streamlined body and good mental strength that gives her an excellent attitude towards work. The jill works with gusto, reliability and dependability, but with her speed comes a lack of stamina. Her high standard of efficiency only lasts for a few hours of constant work. Of course, ferrets can

The base colours of the ferret, the albino and the polecat ferret. (Steven Taylor)

Jill ferrets come in all shapes and sizes. (Steven Taylor)

OPPOSITE: *A range of different-sized hob ferrets. (Steven Taylor)*

work all day if pushed, but they will not work as efficiently when tired. A good ferret glides effortlessly around the warren, disturbing very little other than the rabbits' sleep.

The hob, on the other hand, is a larger and more powerful animal, although the larger head and stronger physique of today's average male ferret are simply too large for successful ferreting, as their size means that they cannot pass through the nets. In addition, fitting the standard ferret-finder collar is difficult and carrying them about is a logistical nightmare. The ferret is now kept better than at any time

in its history, leading to larger and stronger hob ferrets. The hob has a large bearing on the genetic make-up of the litter. Nowadays, ferreters are trying to reduce the size of the hob ferret, not to the minuscule versions that resemble the stoat, but to the ideal size of the average well-proportioned jill ferret, while still retaining the typical mindset of the hob. The hob tends to have the attitude that if the rabbit won't bolt (flee or escape), it will try to persuade it to do so, or alternatively it will stay with the rabbit until the ferreter digs them both out. This is not how everyone likes to go

The polecat ferret, a reference to its colouration and not its genetic make-up. (Steven Taylor)

about things, so if you don't like this attitude, don't work this type of ferret. Once you have worked the same ferret or ferrets for a year or two, you have come to know their characters, strengths and weakness first hand and so can work them accordingly.

There are undoubtedly regional differences in the size of ferrets, the result of generations of ferrets being bred for and adapting to the type of work in their area. The rock-filled Peak District and the Lakes require a smaller ferret, lean enough to fit into the gaps and voids of rocky warrens and stone walls, whereas sandy areas or clay warrens require a larger ferret. While you can work any ferret in any area, a ferret that is too small for the larger tunnels may be overwhelmed, whereas a large ferret will struggle in the tight, confined tunnels of rock, chalk or similar hard substrates.

The main problem with ferrets that are too small is that a rabbit can easily kick them off; they haven't the physical capability to stop a rabbit whilst running around in the pipes. I feel the modern fascination with the so-called greyhound or pencil ferret has changed many ferreters' perceptions about how a modern ferret should be. Some ferreters advocate the inclusion of wild polecat blood into their ferrets' bloodlines, but after experiencing this mix a few times, I don't believe that you will ever beat a well-bred working ferret from pure working domesticated stock.

In the past, these regional differences went largely unnoticed, but with better modes of transport people and their ferrets started to move areas and so these differences gradually became apparent. This has had an impact upon attitudes to breeding specific types of ferret. Whereas once the vast majority of ferrets were bred from any available hob, specific breeding programmes gradually developed that led to the widespread use of suitable hob ferrets for siring litters.

The jill ferret is generally worked more frequently than the hob. Due to her size, she is able to pass through the nets without much disturbance and has a quicker work rate compared to the physically larger hob. Many ferreters like to work small jills, believing them to possess a mystical ability to get behind a rabbit that is stuck in its stop end and so force it to bolt. However, those who have dug a rabbit out of its stop end will know how hard it is to prise out. The shape of the stop end was built by and for the rabbit. If alone, the rabbit's body fits snugly into its excavation with its body gripping the surrounding surface of the tunnel, holding it tight and protecting it from attack. It is impossible for even a small ferret to squeeze past the millimetre's worth of gap between the rabbit and tunnel.

The hob may be a physically slower worker than the quicker jill, but this isn't necessarily a bad thing and as a result the number of ferreters working more hobs than jills is on the increase. With a slower work rate comes the conservation of energy and when this is combined with the hob's focused attitude towards work, you get a slow, methodical worker of consistent efficiency. Jills tend to work in a more manic style, fizzing about the warrens, in the process expending more energy, which impacts upon their endurance and efficiency. However, to an extent the size and sex of the ferret are immaterial – it is the size of the fight inside them that is vitally important.

Both male and female ferrets are affected by hormonal changes coming into the spring period; the hob usually comes into season first. If you do not intend to breed from a hob,

The darker ferret is often overlooked against the greenery of our countryside. (Greg Knight)

it may be a good idea to have him castrated (neutered). Come February and March, the minds of the un-neutered ferrets tend to wander, but the neutered ferret will concentrate on the job in hand. Teams of ferrets, both familiar or strange to each other, will waste valuable time underground either squaring up, ready for a skirmish, or will flirt with each other instead of concentrating on getting the work done. It is unwise to work ferrets of both sexes together whilst in season as it is obvious what the result will be. In certain areas of the UK, working jills in season attract the attention of the wild polecat; I know of several litters over the years that were the results of a union whilst ferreting. A good ferret that knows its job inside out is worth its weight in gold but even these succumb to seasonal 'distractions'.

Before you purchase your ferrets, you must decide what combination you intend to keep and how many of each. You can maintain your ferrets in courts of jills only, hobs only, or a combination of both. I usually keep all of my ferrets (jills and hobs) together in one court. Throughout the winter they live in harmony, but I have to act swiftly prior to the spring and summer breeding season, separating the entire (non-neutered) hobs and leaving only the castrated and vasectomized hobs in with the jills. Without swift action, you will end up with a litter of young ferrets (kits); it is surprising and rather saddening to hear just how many young ferrets are born this way, through ignorance of basic husbandry.

PURCHASING A FERRET

One of the most important but often most frustrating aspects of ferreting is the purchasing of ferrets. It is unfortunate that not all ferrets will work and that is why I have included a few words of warning to try to avoid the pitfalls that have caught out many a ferreter. You should never buy a ferret on a whim or at a show, as you will not have the slightest idea about its background. Think carefully before you buy any ferret – check

out the homes, the parents and the state of their welfare, as opposed to the convenience of just buying any ferret from any background when it is available. Resist the temptation of falling for the tale of the ready-made, tried and tested ferret. If a ferret was that good, why would anyone want to part with it? It is preferable to start with a youngster bought from a reputable source, as you will know it hasn't got any secret bad habits lurking in its history.

Picking the right ferret is just the start. Like all animals, its upbringing will play a large part in its future habits, both good and bad. The best age to purchase a ferret is undoubtedly when it is between seven and nine weeks of age. A kit (a young ferret under sixteen weeks of age) is at an age when you can raise it in the desired manner without any fear of it having already acquired too many bad habits. The reason why so many people purchase a youngster over an adult is of course its teeth. The teeth and jaws of a youngster are undeveloped so therefore do not have the power or sharpness of an adult and this will be noticeable when you start to train it in the ways of being handled.

THE YOUNG FERRET

Ferrets are usually born in the late spring/early summer, are weaned at around six weeks of age and then are generally rehomed at between seven and nine weeks of age. When properly reared, these youngsters will start to work slowly about November time, although, like every animal, some will be naturals while others will require a bit longer to get used to the reality of being a working ferret. Remember, how you treat these animals up to the end of their first working season will shape the rest of their working lives. Bad habits are easily made and take time to correct, if at all. A lot of ferreters fall into the trap of

OPPOSITE: *Future hopes and expectations are always high for young ferrets, though not all of them will make the grade. (Steven Taylor)*

giving precedence to the ferret that seems to be working best, thus not giving experience to another youngster that really needs it. Not all ferrets will work to your standards, so a degree of weeding out will occur, although I have moved on a ferret or two myself only to see a year or two later that they have evolved into first-class workers for their new owners. Unfortunately, this happens from time to time to everyone who works with animals.

HANDLING

There is nothing more comical than a hutch full of ferret kits, all as mad as a box of frogs. Their naivety, youthful exuberance and energy ensure that they will spend large amounts of time mimicking their hunting skills on each other. It looks far worse than it is and is a vital part of their upbringing. But play-fighting and using their teeth on each other

To pick up a ferret is simplicity itself. (Steven Taylor)

is one thing; using them on your hands is a definite no-no.

The ferret is an animal that needs to be handled, stroked and played with as much possible. Getting them used to your hands is *the* most important part of their welfare, for without the ability to pick up the ferret, how are you going to clean out their housing, never mind go ferreting? There are several methods of getting the ferret out of its nippy stage. The method I use has served me and my friends well over the years and although I am open to seeing new methods, I am amazed at some of the methods people have tried to convince me will work. One misconception is that all ferrets are born biters. This is utter nonsense. If the parents have been well-handled, fed and looked after, the genes inside the youngsters will carry the same traits. Young ferrets do not know right from wrong or the difference between a hand and a playmate or chunk of food, so in the following weeks and months you will be educating the kits about what is acceptable.

To get the ferret used to being handled, you must accept that both your and the ferret's patience will be tested, as you are dealing with a little immature animal, just like a pup. Ferrets, like all animals, will detect the slightest nerves or hesitancy, so you must always pick them up in one swoop. Never play about in front of the ferret, pulling your hand to and fro, as this will just encourage the kit to jump and hang on with its teeth to the first thing it meets, which will be your hand. Talk calmly to the ferret as you pick it up.

To pick the ferret up is simplicity itself. Picking it up from the stomach area, between the front and rear legs, a kit will be resting in the palm of your hands, but if you are uncertain of its likely reaction or if it is a adult ferret, you can hold it around the neck, secure in the knowledge that it cannot turn around and bite you in such a hold. To hold a ferret safely in such a hold, you pick the ferret up by putting your thumb and forefinger gently around the ferret's neck and the three remaining fingers behind the front legs and around

the stomach area of the ferret. You should get the ferret used to being picked up in as many different ways as possible – place it on the ground, play with it and pick it up lots of times, as you need your ferret to be used to any eventuality whilst out ferreting..

The method I use to stop ferrets nipping is as follows. Play with the ferret as if you were a fellow ferret. Rough it up a little, tickle its stomachs or its ears and it will react by trying to bite you, quite normal for any youngster. When it goes to strike, either gently pinch its nose or gently flick it with your finger in order to shock the ferret. You are sending out the message that you are not there to be bitten. Other methods practised to eradicate biting include forcing a knuckle inside the ferret's mouth, or simply handling the ferret and ignoring the nips, but, with this latter method, one day the adult will bite and it will hurt. Better to have a ferret that is bullet-proof than to be always thinking it may bite, which will undermine your confidence and the ferret will pick up on this.

Once a ferret is at the stage where it does not go for the strike, I put a little spittle or milk on my finger and let the ferret lick it off. When the liquid has gone, it is natural for the youngster to have a nibble. Again, repeat the gentle tap or flick to the nose. In my opinion, this isn't cruel, but is what we must do in order to get the ferret to associate biting human beings with discomfort and to enable us to have a working relationship with it. I have been criticized by those who regard this method as being somewhat barbaric. Their preferred method is to play with the ferret and just let it bite. When it does, and believe me it will, they hold the ferret up to head height, look it in the eye and say in a stern voice 'no'. This apparently stops the ferret from biting again. This method has never worked for me, but you can make up your own mind as to its effectiveness.

Do not forget, though, that the rate at which the ferret grows from a little eight-week-old kit to a full physical specimen at eighteen weeks is quick. The mental growth comes

All ferrets must be accustomed to having their handlers standing over them and being picked up without reacting. (Steven Taylor)

later, but trying to get a sixteen-week-old ferret to stop nipping is a lot harder and more painful, due to a set of fully grown teeth, than with a smaller, weaker youngster, so don't leave this job too late.

TRAINING

Ferrets require very little in the way of training, as their method of working is instinctive. Reinforcing this instinct by feeding the kits rabbit with its fur left on gets them accustomed to the smell, taste and texture of the rabbit. Correct handling from a young age will ensure that when they are getting overexcited on their first few trips, you should be able to pick your ferrets up without any accidents.

With daily handling, the ferret will grow up realizing that the hand isn't on the menu. Accidents will happen, especially with excited youngsters, but this is no excuse – a bite is still a bite.

It is a good idea to get a ferret used to the ferret-finder collar before its first ferreting trip. By placing a collar on the ferret for short spells of time at home many weeks before it goes ferreting, it will adjust to the strange sensation of wearing the collar. This helps to reduce the time the ferret spends trying to rub off the collar, especially when it should be concentrating on finding rabbits.

One aspect of training often overlooked is getting the ferrets used to being stood over before they are picked up. Whilst ferreting, the novice ferret will experience a mixture of excitement and nervousness and when approached to be picked up it can often dart back down a hole if it is not used to being handled in this way.

This is a far more common problem than many would like to admit to. The ferret is a very small animal that has just been placed in an environment that is a world away from its hutch or run. The experiences it has just encountered will excite as much as frighten it, and this is when your training pays off. It is vital that the ferret gets accustomed to being picked up in as many different ways as possible, taught to go in, through and out of the pipes that make up a warren, but, most importantly, it must be used to being picked up from the ground. Put yourself in the position of the ferret and imagine what it looks like to be stood over by a giant whose hand is reaching down towards you. By acclimatizing a ferret to this action, it will not be intimidated by the approaching hand and will react well when coming out of the warren. Too many ferreters are impatient and grab a ferret when it refuses to clear the hole. This is a sure-fire way to getting a ferret to 'skulk'. Skulking is when the ferret will appear at the mouth of a hole and refuse to come within arms' reach, instead going back down the hole, simply to reappear once you have retreated. These youngsters need coaxing out, gently and calmly, and with practice and experience they will improve. If you aim to see things from the ferrets' perspective as well as your own, you will begin to understand how to avoid instilling bad habits in the young ferret.

The carrying box is another object that requires familiarization, but this is done by simply placing the ferrets in the box whilst cleaning out their hutch at home. All being well, once the calendar has reached its eleventh month, the young ferrets should be ready for work.

COMING INTO SEASON

As the winter turns towards spring, the ferrets will come into season. The physical signs of a ferret in season are obvious. The hob is usually first; his testicles will drop while his aroma will increase. The jill's vulva will swell and she will stay in season until mated or given an injection by a veterinary surgeon, or she will naturally come out of season around September. The breeding season of the ferret is governed by the hours of daylight over the hours of darkness (photoperiodism). Both sexes will exhibit different characteristics due to the hormone imbalance.

One of the many old wives' tales connected with ferreting states that if you don't breed from a jill she will die. The act of mating (coitus) stops the build-up of oestrogen; it is this act and not the birth of the litter that removes the ferret from her season. If you do not want a litter, you can remove the jill from her season by using a vasectomized hob ferret (hoblet). If a hoblet is not available a jill-jab is available from the veterinary surgeon that will have the same effect of removing the jill from her season. The jill usually comes into season twice a year and sometimes the removal – by whatever method – can result in a phantom pregnancy, resulting in all the characteristics of a real pregnancy (nest-making, producing milk, broodiness and character/mood swings), but without the litter of kits.

Neutering

Neutering is the only completely effective way of preventing any unwanted litters and fights between inmates, and of reducing the aroma of the summertime hob. At a time when a lot more ferreters are utilizing the working hob, neutered hobs (hobbles) can be kept with each other and with jills for the full year without the usual scraps, scrapes and pregnancies that will otherwise result. Sometimes confusion arises when taking a ferret to the vet to have an operation such as a vasectomy, or to be castrated. An entire hob is one that is left naturally alone; he will come into season and has the capability to breed with an in-season jill ferret, and get aggressive with other in-season hobs. A hoblet is a hob ferret that has been vasectomized. He acts exactly the same as an entire male ferret (hob) and can take the in-season jill out of season by mating with her, but because he has had a vasectomy, he is unable to get her pregnant. A hobble is a castrated male ferret. Having had his testicles removed he is incapable of breeding. Hobbles generally live in harmony the whole year round with both hobs and jills.

With the increased awareness of the importance of the jill's season, the use of a vasectomized hob is becoming the popular way of removing the jill from her season. After a simple operation and a quarantine time of around six weeks, this hoblet can remove a lot of jills from their seasons during the summer months, proving a lot more cost-effective than

It is important for young ferrets to be accustomed to the smell, taste and texture of rabbit before their first encounter whilst at work. (Steven Taylor)

the jill-jab. There has been a lot of controversy concerning the jills' season and the thorny subject of removing them from it, but I feel you cannot take any risks with your ferrets' health. How would you feel if your jills succumbed to the grim reaper a few weeks before you were due to start ferreting just because you had done nothing about their season?

THE FERRET'S DIET

When you decide to go ferreting, it is necessary to plan your ferrets' feeding regime to gain maximum efficiency and results. This will depend upon the workload ahead, the warrens and their positions, the amount of hours spent working and the time of year you are ferreting. You will need to feed your ferrets to suit the day ahead.

In the past, the ferret's diet has been, well, not the best, but it hasn't always been bread and milk slops as popularly assumed. In several old readings I have found evidence of the

ferret being fed meat or meat scraps, their natural diet. Nowadays, some owners advocate free-feeding, which I am sure works well for them and their ferrets, but the more I compare notes with different ferreters, the more I am coming to the conclusion that the best method is in direct comparison with feeding a hawk, that is, to feed to suit the day ahead, as noted above. After practising both free-feeding and specific feeding for a few years, I have learnt from my own experiences which best suits my methods and ferrets. However, the individuality of ferrets and ferreters ensures that what suits me will not necessarily suit you, so if you are happy with your personal set-up and arrangements, stay with them.

There is a world of difference between feeding to suit the needs of the day and starvation. The object is to have a keen, enthusiastic and fit ferret for the work ahead, not a weakened, famished one. If you starve an animal for any length of time, it dies, simple as that. In the past, the ferret was fed a poor diet at home, so that when it came across succulent meat under the ground it couldn't resist it, but the end result would be counter-productive, as the ferret would gorge itself and then sleep it off.

Today, the ferret is fed a quality diet of fresh rabbit in the winter months or twelve months of the year if possible. The ferret thus becomes accustomed to the smell, taste and texture of the rabbit, so that when they meet underground, they are no longer strangers. What happens to many ferrets when they have been denied this regular experience with the rabbit, especially with its jacket on, is that they do not fully understand just what a rabbit is and what it means. Instinct will drive the ferret on to hunt, but when the rabbit is cornered in a stop end, for instance, if the ferret does not truly understand that the rabbit is its quarry it will go through the motions and eventually come off the live rabbit as the incentive isn't there.

Once the ferret truly understands what the rabbit is, it will try to bolt it, sticking with it and trying to kill it. If successful, the ferret doesn't stay there and eat the rabbit, it simply moves on in search of others. However, take the same dead rabbit and put it in the ferrets' hutch or court and they are on it like a shoal of piranhas. The well-trained and fed ferret seems to understand the nature of the rabbit in different environments. Of course, ferrets will sometimes start to eat the soft tissue on a recently killed rabbit, such as the eyes or the area of neck it has bitten to kill the rabbit, but on the whole, they move on in search of more prey. In order to carry out successfully the regime of feeding for the day ahead, you must know your ferrets. Too little food and they will fade over the coming hours; too much and they will just go through the motions and miss that extra nip required to perform to their full potential.

The complete ferret (pellet) food is a revolutionary breakthrough for the ferrets' needs, especially in the warmer months when flies can cause havoc with raw meat. The invention of dried food has given us a healthy and nutritional alternative if required, especially enabling the ferret to be enjoyed as a pet without the owners having to feed, handle or store raw meat, but it is not a substitute for the working ferret's natural diet, the rabbit. My personal experiences have led me to feed pellets when necessary in the summer months, but when I can, and especially with the young kits, I feed the rabbit in all its glory, fur, meat and bone.

When feeding the ferrets, the amount of food is governed by the number of ferrets kept and their level of activity, as a more active animal will eat more. The ferret requires a balanced and high-quality diet, which usually is either a complete dry food specially designed for ferrets or a raw meat-based diet (rabbit, pigeon and so on) or a combination of the two. If feeding one of the many ferret complete diets (biscuit), follow the feeding guidelines on the packaging but remember that these are guides only. Although some ferrets are smaller than others, a half a mug full of ferret food in a plastic bowl should be suffice for two ferrets a day. The food will be eaten over many sittings and is fed ad lib, but if you notice some ferrets, especially hobs, sitting by the bowl and eating too much, just feed and remove the food after a couple of hours. Biscuit does appear to put a little more weight on a ferret than rabbit meat, due to the rabbit's natural leanness.

If feeding rabbit to your ferrets, a couple of ferrets would only require the equivalent of a leg and a half a day, or a similar amount of diced rabbit. It is common to feed raw meat to ferrets at night in the warmer weather, to cut down on the flies: this is why many feed biscuit during the summer and meat during the winter. If feeding raw meat, check for hidden food, as ferrets will often hide some to eat later and these pieces are what the flies will be attracted to. Pregnant or nursing jills should be given as much food as they are eating, which can be as much as a single prepared rabbit a day if a large litter has started to eat solid food. It is amazing how much food a large litter of ferrets and their mother will eat during the course of twenty-four hours.

Each ferret is individual in its mental and physical make up. Whatever your feeding practice, ensure it suits the ferrets' needs and not just your own convenience. Some ferrets do better on one food than another, some eat more than others due to a different metabolism, and all these factors require constant attention in order to get the balance right. If you are contemplating changes in the ferrets' diet, I advise doing it gradually over a few days.

Whatever feeding regime you choose, you must ensure that the ferrets have access to plenty of clean drinking water. If you are feeding dried food, the ferrets' intake of water will be very high when compared to that of rabbit-fed ferrets, as rabbit meat has a high moisture content. Water is usually delivered in two ways. In hutches, the gravity-fed drinking bottle is used, and in a court, a gravity-fed poultry drinker. The water must be checked and replenished so as to avoid a build-up of algae inside the water holder. If you do get a build-up of algae in a bottle there is a simple way of cleaning it out. Fill the bottle to about a quarter with water, insert two tablespoons of sand, place your thumb over the top and shake well, rinse, then fill with clean water ready for the lid to be replaced. The water bottle will be like new once again. Care must be taken during any bouts of cold weather, as frost will block up the bottle's spout and could crack old plastic bottles.

The choice is yours as to whether you feed an ad-lib or a selective diet to your ferrets. If I am working all week, I work one team of ferrets and at the end of the day they are fed and the next day another team is employed, and so on. This gives me time to feed one team whilst the other is fed a fraction of their normal food. After working, breeding and watching my ferrets grow, I have no doubts that this method is a sure-fire way of ensuring that the maximum potential of the working ferret is achieved.

HOUSING

Ferret housing has changed so much that nowadays their homes resemble palaces compared with the shoebox hutches of years gone by. The spare space, number of ferrets you keep and whether you want a hutch or a court system will dictate the ferrets' housing. Whatever you choose, you must ensure that it is not only right for your ferrets but also for you, as you're the one who has to clean it out. The housing is the centre of your ferrets' world and when they are not working it must stimulate their mental and physical needs. We don't like to live in squalid, cramped conditions and neither do the ferrets. If you intend only to keep a couple of ferrets, a large hutch tends to be the favoured choice, ranging from 5ft (1.5m) or 6ft (1.8m) long by 18 × 18in (46 × 46cm). Many hutches have a run underneath to double the floor space without doubling the area taken up in the garden. However, the popular choice is fast becoming the ferret court. The ferret court can be any size. It consists of an aviary-type building situated on concrete or paving slabs to prevent escapees and has a housing area that protects the ferret from the elements, be they sun, wind, rain or snow.

CHAPTER TWO

The Ferreter's Quarry: The Rabbit

In my opinion, the rabbit (*Oryctolagus cuniculus*) is the definitive survivor. Mankind has tried everything in a bid to curtail its existence, ranging from the ferret, rifle, gun, net, wire, trap, dog and gas to the introduction of the disease, myxomatosis. Whilst overcoming all of these obstacles, the rabbit still has to

face the threat posed by the millions of motorcars which kill and maim a large percentage of Britain's wild rabbit population. As ferreters, it is our duty to control the presence of rabbits down to a manageable, economic and realistic level which suits both us and the person on whose land we are ferreting. After spending

The rabbit, the ultimate survivor. (Greg Knight)

A rabbit is still a rabbit, irrespective of its size, shape or colour. (Greg Knight)

the majority of my life learning to curtail its population, I greatly respect the rabbit and will try to do it the justice it deserves within the pages of this chapter.

The present UK rabbit population in 2007 has been estimated at forty-five million, rising annually by 2 per cent and causing upwards of a conservatively estimated £150 million worth of damage to the environment each year. In 2002, this figure was £115 million, with a cost of controlling the UK's rabbit population of £5 million. The cost of damage doesn't include the costs involved in controlling the rabbits and repairing their damage, because it would be almost impossible to establish these figures.

When I am on my travels, I constantly meet with folk who talk of exterminating the rabbit in certain locations, but this is an impossible aim. Mankind has had at his disposal many creditable and successful methods of control, which, when combined, can make serious inroads into the local rabbit population, but they still return year after year, regrouping in enough numbers to ensure that those who control them mustn't be too complacent. Complacency breeds contempt and there is no place in this book or in my presence for contempt when dealing with the rabbit. Those of us that control the lagomorphs have a deep-rooted respect for this creature and therefore it is our duty to ensure that each rabbit is duly dispatched as humanely and efficiently as possible, to ensure that there is no cruelty in our countryside.

In order to maximize our chances of success, we need to study and understand the life of our quarry and its habitat. The rabbit warren is the ferrets' and ferreters' place of work. It is vital that we understand how each different warren is constructed, why certain sections are dangerous to a ferret and why we must never underestimate the potential dangers that any warren could present at any given time.

Opinion of the rabbit is divided. To many, it is a popular pet with a charming and cuddly character, but to others it is the baby-faced assassin of the fields, causing millions of pounds worth of damage. On the other hand, it saves on maintenance of roadside verges and forestry clearings as it crops the grass. It also creates new ecosystems, enabling birds such as the stone curlew to nest successfully and survive, while providing food for all of its predators (including humans). But while the rabbit may appear 'cute and cuddly', nothing could be further from the truth in the case of the wild rabbit, for underneath a cleverly adapted package of fur, teeth and sharp claws we have an animal that will do anything to protect its own species in its battle for survival. Cannibalistic tendencies are not uncommon, especially when very young rabbits are encountered by the older bucks from the dominant group of the warren.

Rabbits also quickly force their young out into the harsh environment of the outside world in readiness to produce another litter. The survival of the fittest is a harsh reality that all rabbits must face, especially when, increasingly, trees are being replaced by concrete and hedges by fences, although the rabbit is fast adapting to this urban-based environment.

THE HISTORY OF THE RABBIT IN THE UK

Although it feels like the rabbit has been a part of our land since time began, it hasn't. It was introduced into this country approximately 800 years ago by the Normans for food and fur, but the unreliable enclosure constructions at the time meant that many escaped and set about gradually populating the UK. Initially, the rabbit made the most of what was then a sparsely inhabited island and when humans

cleared any woodland the rabbits moved in. The rabbit population remained fairly stable until the 1845 General Enclosure Act, which allowed landowners to enclose common land without reference to Parliament, and then it exploded!

The various Enclosure Acts passed during this period enabled the landowners to take control of common land, planting thousands of hedgerows up and down the country and changing the landscape forever. Land was being cleared from forestry to open farmland and the newly planted hedges formed a series of shelters from predators and with all the disturbed earth, digging warrens was a lot easier. The land was sown and harvested more efficiently due to the growth in technology and farming techniques and was used for cereal production, especially winter crops, just as it is to this day. For the rabbits, food was easier to access and when you add this to the easier housing, the population began to grow. In addition, as our technology in society became greater, the way in which we hunted changed. Firearms were now advancing and with this came the upsurge in grand sporting estates and farms. Gamekeepers and such folk were protecting the game birds and this meant that these birds' predators were being controlled. Large-scale control of the fox, stoat and birds of prey meant that the rabbit was allowed to feed, breed and thrive like never before. The rabbit soon become a major pest and with so much damage reported to Parliament, it had to act. Various laws were brought in.

When the Ground Game Act came into force in 1880, it made it possible for any tenant to hunt the rabbit. Previously it had been only the rich and the noble who could legally hunt the rabbit without fear of prosecution. By the turn of the twentieth century, up to 100 million rabbits were being caught annually, but the population was still growing so more laws were brought, designating the whole of England and Wales as a rabbit-clearance area and giving all landowners an obligation to control the rabbits on their land. The Prevention of Damage by Rabbits Act 1939 was closely followed by the Agricultural Act 1947 and the Prevention of Damage by Pests Act 1949. The government of the early 1950s estimated the population at 60 million rabbits, causing an estimated £50 million pounds worth of damage. Further control measures were discussed and the Pests Act 1954 was introduced.

We now know, with hindsight, that the country was about to be hit by a disease called myxomatosis, which would change the UK's perception of the rabbit forever. From 1850 to 1950 the population peaked at 60 million, but then myxomatosis hit and reduced their numbers to just 600,000. More than fifty years later, we still have this disease infecting our land, albeit a weaker strain, but it has left people reluctant to eat the meat of our own wild rabbit. Although the present population of rabbits is estimated at 45 million, it is rising quickly, though I personally doubt we will ever see the rabbit back to the pre-myxomatosis numbers of 60 million, due to the direct result of man's inability to leave nature alone and the volume of people who now control the rabbits.

The rabbit is a great adapter to its surrounding environment; this Isle of Lundy rabbit is protected against the harsh wind. (Nigel Housden/Pinsharp Photography)

RABBIT BIOLOGY

The rabbit belongs to the order *Lagomorpha*, a family that is distributed in almost every part of the UK on a variety of terrain up to a height of 2,000ft (600m) above sea level. The rabbit is often found in areas of poor-quality vegetation. To gain the maximum nutritional benefits from this limited diet, the rabbit will pass the majority of its food (80 per cent) twice through its digestive system. It first breaks down the food and releases all of the nutrients into the bloodstream. While the rabbit is resting or having a break from feeding midway through the night, it will pass a first faecal dropping. Although dark and round like the ordinary droppings we usually see, these droppings are soft, moist and covered in mucus. The softer dropping is very rarely seen, as the rabbit immediately eats them again. The final droppings that we see are the resulting parts of food that are indigestible. This system allows rabbits to stay underground with their own food supply, so that, if need be, they can stay underground all day and night through bad weather, against danger of predation, or if there is a large disturbance such as a major clearance around the warrens that spooks the residents.

The rabbit may be aesthetically pleasing to look at, but the whole body has been designed to protect it from the climate and its predators. The fur, which protects the body from the elements, has a dense, soft undercoat through which the longer outer coat protrudes. The coat is obviously a lot denser during the winter months with the colour usually a greyish-brown, but local populations can vary from the albino to jet black in colour. I have only once seen a wild albino rabbit and whilst feeding with its normal-coloured siblings it become another fixture in my game bag, as did the countless ginger, black or whatever coloured rabbits I have encountered. I cannot afford the luxury of taking the colour of a rabbit into account; a rabbit is a rabbit at the end of the day.

The rabbit has those legendary big radars (ears) situated on the side of its head with the ability to turn independently, scanning the area for alien noises in two separate directions at the same time if required. These sounds alert the rabbit to possible attack from its enemies, the predators that include us humans. Just like our hounds casting into the wind for scent, the rabbit also casts its nose and ears into the breeze because it isn't just scent that travels in the wind but noise as well. The whiskers on its nose can detect and sense the taste of its surroundings and the smell of its opponents. All of these senses then translate into an alarm bell. The rear legs are longer than the front pair and are used to pound the earth in alarm, which is reminiscent of the drummer signalling to the troops in the past, hence the rabbit's nickname of 'the drummer'.

The rear legs are big and powerful for another reason. They provide the legendary power and speed that the rabbit needs for extra quick acceleration to escape from danger. The short, sharp sprint to cover or out of danger is the rabbit's best source of protection. On its feet, the rabbit has a coating of extra thick hair which ensures it has a good grip on even the slipperiest of surfaces; add those large sharp claws and the rabbit has the capability to punch hard with razor sharp weapons at its enemies and own kind during its battle for survival.

The eyes are situated on either side of a narrow head, providing an excellent viewpoint of nearly every angle. The teeth, both upper and lower incisors, can cut a smooth 45-degree cut. Animals such as the deer lack the upper incisor and so leave a ragged edge to the top of their cut, which is a good way of telling the difference between rabbit and deer damage on trees. To finish off nature's perfect bundle of fur, we have the nice white tail, which either alerts the other rabbits with its alarm signal, or tell us that we have missed another bolt-hole as he runs off to educate his friends of our whereabouts.

A healthy rabbit, despite its unusual teeth. (Steven Taylor)

There isn't a calendar month that goes by when we do not see evidence of baby rabbits. (Nigel Housden / Pinsharp Photography)

The Rabbit's Ability to Breed

The rabbit's other survival mechanism is its famous ability to breed, which is assisted by a combination of factors. Rabbits are generally able to breed at a young age, often four or five times a year because the gestation period is only twenty-eight to thirty-one days. In addition, females (does) experience induced ovulation, which means that they release eggs in response to copulation rather than according to a regular cycle. They may also conceive immediately after a litter has been born.

The breeding season of the rabbit in the UK has changed. No longer is it confined to the months of February to July, but occurs over the whole twelve months of the year due to the change in our climate, although the peak times are still the summer months. There isn't a calendar month that goes by when we do not see evidence of baby rabbits, be it inside the pregnant rabbit, fresh nesting showing imminent birth, or young rabbits of varying ages. I predict that in the next four years and beyond the signs will only grow stronger.

The rabbit has its young in what is called a stop, but nests of varying ages can be found close to each other in the main warrens, albeit on the outskirts of the tunnel system. Consisting of fresh bedding, this is where the youngsters' lives begin and where they are wholly dependent upon their mother for food and to protect them from predators, fellow rabbits competing for survival and the elements. Unlike the rat, however, which will protect its young to the death, the rabbit is a bit of a coward when mothering and will bolt freely when with young, as opposed to not bolting whilst carrying young. I suspect that the survival instinct to flee is stronger in the alert mother, diverting attention away from the young, whereas the pregnant rabbit knows that the chances of outrunning a predator are slim, so reaching the safety of the stop provides the best chance of survival.

The youngsters are born blind, with an average litter being between two and five, but going by the amount of nests I have dug, I would say three is the probable average. At about ten days their ears open, their eyes shortly afterwards and at about three weeks, they start to venture out. At one month, they are weaned off their mother, who may already be pregnant again. The rabbit reaches sexual maturity at the age of three to four months, so the early-born rabbits are well capable of producing a litter the very same year. By using a modern version of the Fibonacci sequence, a mathematical conundrum, the resulting offspring can be calculated, not taking into consideration the loss to predation and natural mortality. It just goes to show that however hard we control these animals, they have the ability to replenish their population in no time at all.

THE RABBIT'S DIET

To support a rabbit population, whatever the size, the land must meet certain criterion: food; cover for protection; and suitable earth in which to build a warren. Although the rabbit can and indeed does travel some distance for quality food, it needs a good supply close to home. Good food is essential to support the young rabbits in their important first few months of life. During certain times of the year, the rabbit will on occasions travel great distances to feed, especially when the fields are turned over in preparation for drilling or have been sprayed with chemicals, making a lot of the crops temporarily inedible. If the weather is wet or damp in the early months of the year, many young rabbits will succumb to exposure in the wetter environment. With constant grazing, however, the rabbits can evolve an area into prime rabbit ground, enabling the dangers of such wet conditions to be vastly reduced.

The weather affects all animals, so the rabbit has developed a feeding system (*see* above) to help overcome any potential threat to its survival from extreme conditions. The rabbit requires a certain amount of cover close

Over 90 per cent of juvenile rabbits die before maturity, most within their first three weeks of life. (Author)

It doesn't always take a lot of rabbits to create a lot of damage. (Steven Taylor)

to its home to give it extra protection from predators. We must remember that we are not the only predator after the rabbit, so it has evolved its survival instincts to recognize what endangers its existence and has evolved survival strategies to combat whatever the danger may be.

The rabbit's diet is rich and varied, but you will notice that certain plants are always situated around the warrens. These tend to be plants that the rabbit dislikes and will not eat, such as ragwort, nettle and hemlock, to name just a few. Because the rabbit passes food through its digestive system twice, it only needs to be out grazing for as long as it takes to eat enough to fill its stomach once a day. The rabbit will first feed when coming above ground and then, when full, will rest, enjoy the sun or do what rabbits do. Rabbits are not only selective grazers, choosing the best and most nutritional plants and seedlings, but with the resident farm stock helping,

they can change the look of the surrounding pastures in little or no time, causing major land damage. The estimated rabbit damage in 2006 was £150 million, with the potential to double if the ratio of surviving youngsters changes for any reason. Watching a litter of young rabbits eat away at the edge of a field is the equivalent of having a few pairs of scissors constantly cutting the top off a valuable crop.

The buck and doe weigh between 2–4.5lb (1–2kg) each and have the potential to eat up to 25 per cent of their weight in greens every day. When the rabbits move away from the safety of their warren in search of food, the greater the amount of damage that can be achieved in a smaller amount of time. Travelling a field or two in search of higher-quality food is quite normal for most rabbits. There are not many crops that the rabbit doesn't like. It has been calculated that a field of winter wheat can be hit with a loss of 1 per cent of its yield per hectare, at a estimated cost of £7.50 per rabbit;

The sap of a tree is a much-liked delicacy of the rabbit. (Nigel Housden / Pinsharp Photography)

on spring barley, the damage is less at 0.5 per cent (£3.90 per rabbit). It may not sound a lot, but when it results in a loss of 143lb (65kg) of wheat per rabbit based on the number of ears lost and the loss of grain per ear, it certainly brings the severity home. Diversity of crops has simply brought diversity to the rabbit's diet, as those farmers who have lost their maize game covers will testify. According to the Department for Environment, Food and Rural Affairs (DEFRA), rabbit damage is estimated during trials at selective farms and analysed by scientists at the government's Central Science Laboratory (CSL), where the comparisons between protected and un-

protected fields are made. In 1ha (2.5-acre) enclosures, a number of known rabbits are kept in a climate of different crops. Keeping rabbits in a small area overcomes the difficulty of estimating the population over large tracts of land, as the cost per rabbit can be accurately diagnosed in the smaller pens. Equal numbers of does and bucks enable a stable population and in areas up to 50ha (123.5 acres), the scientists can represent the densities experienced elsewhere in the UK. Such trials provide an opportunity for DEFRA to show the cost per rabbit ratio and this is important for two reasons. The first is to see if rabbit control is cost-effective and the second, and to me most important, reason is to show that the more rabbits resident, the greater the financial damage!

THE RABBIT WARREN

The warren serves two main purposes for the rabbit, providing a home and thus shelter from the elements, but it also gives a degree of safety from the majority of the rabbit's predators that are too large to enter. Inside the warren there may be dozens of rabbits, depending on the size of their home, or just a single or couple, a buck and a doe. Generally, there are more does than bucks and with the larger warrens, each warren is generally split up into sub-warrens, which have their own hierarchy, including the dominant bucks and does.

The tunnel system that forms a warren can range from small to the larger pipes, depending on the soil structure. Many of the pipes have a bottle-like structure in the middle, which allows the rabbits to pass through when in danger or high activity. The soil condition or type dictates how the warren is constructed and the pipes usually follow the looser or softer substrates; if the softer soil drops suddenly, so do the pipes, which can go down vertically and cause a problem for the smaller ferret.

Once down in this shaft, the rabbit can squeeze itself up by using its back to touch the back of the pipe and manoeuvre itself up, but the ferret hasn't got the body size to do so, causing it to be trapped. The heavier soil also allows the rabbit to dig deeper without fear of collapses. The deeper the tunnels, the longer it will take the ferrets to explore and work them, giving the rabbit more time to find an exit or one of its stop ends. This is when you will require more than one ferret on the job. The warrens are usually built in the driest areas, but with the way the climate is changing, the water table rises at an alarming rate so it is common for some of these warrens to become waterlogged. Resident rabbits will use these pipes in emergencies,

As the ferret's body width is a lot smaller than the rabbit's, it is easy for it to become trapped in a vertical shaft.

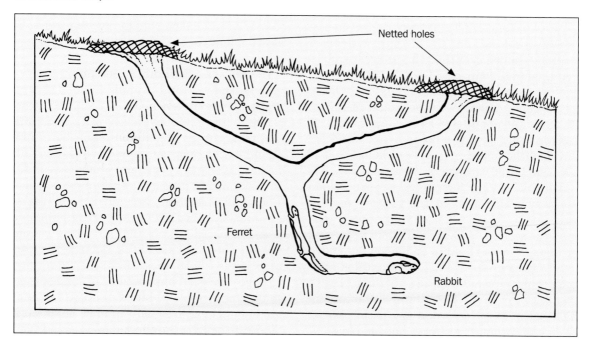

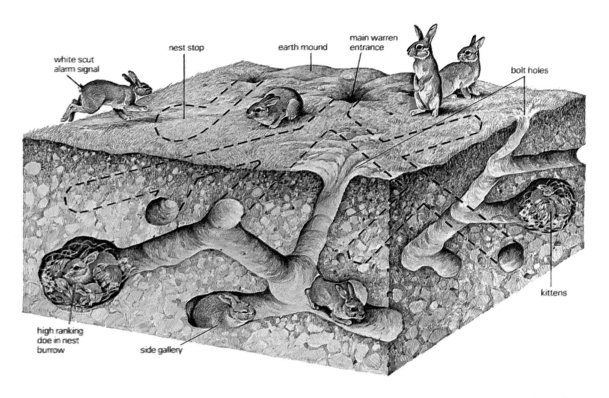

The ferreter's place of work, the rabbit warren. (Eaglemoss Publications Ltd / The Hayward Art Group)

as a lot of ferrets will not pursue the rabbit through deep water.

The warren is randomly constructed, usually with the does doing the digging, with extra workings added over the years to create a labyrinth of interconnected tunnels that serve to confuse the ferret and other predators, whereas the rabbit knows every nook and cranny of its home and definitely has the upper hand. A warren could have two holes or two hundred, but don't be fooled by a lack of holes as it is the amount of yardage of the tunnels that is important. Large warrens may also include many sub-warrens and these form another part of the rabbit's defence. Just a single pipe may connect the sub-warrens, but this could be enough to reach up to and beyond a 100yd (91m) stretch of warrens. The hardest warrens to ferret tend to be the single hole with plenty of yardage underground and many inhabitants. With only one means of escape, the ferret will most certainly bottle up a great

deal in stops, running the risk of killing underground and getting blocked in, so the use of an electronic ferret-finder system is essential (for details of this product, *see* Chapter 5).

To give the maximum protection to its occupiers, the warren has many hidden escape shafts and exits (bolt-holes), all dug from inside so no visible mounds of soil are noticeable from the outside. These bolt-holes are legendary for being hidden in the long grass, bushes and especially under dead leaves. To further confuse its enemies, the rabbit sometimes leaves a pipe unfinished, stopping a few inches from the surface. The result of such a construction is that a bolting rabbit will hit the shaft end with enough force to open it out, with the rabbit then bursting through the soil and becoming an escapee unless you possess a good ferreting dog as a partner. These partially hidden holes may also be caused by the earth being turned over after the harvest, or a hole becoming partially filled in for some reason.

You also may have noticed that a large majority of bolt-holes go down vertically. This is done so that when the rabbit bolts out above ground, it shoots up into the air to confuse the predator chasing it. If an animal is small enough to chase them underground into the warren, it is usually too small to actually jump straight out of the vertical shaft, unlike the larger rabbit.

When outside their warren, the rabbits employ a vigilant defence mechanism based on a theory that cannot be faulted – the more rabbits out feeding, the more eyes, ears and noses there are on the look-out for danger. The greater the number, the less time the individual spends looking for danger and the more time can be spent consuming food. Just sit back and watch the rabbit in a field and you will see how the rabbit uses the same runs out into a particular area and, when out, it will every so often interrupt its grazing, lifting its head up to survey its surroundings. It may also decide to sit up on its back legs to give it a better vantage point. These rabbit runs are often the downfall of a well-hidden warren under a large thick bush or buildings. Sometimes when running for freedom using these runs, if the water was rising, they would still paddle through to try and avoid capture. Often, many ferreters will not take into account the rabbit's willingness to swim, climb or run the gauntlet, often resulting in many escapees.

The rabbit feeding in the middle of a large area or near a hedgerow will be on a high state of alertness, as it knows it is open to attack in either situation, with the open spaces being ideal for the fast predator, or the hedgerow providing cover for an ambush. Totally reliant upon each other, the rabbit informs its colleagues of danger with stout kicks into the ground, which not only tell the surface rabbits of danger, but the vibrations inform the subterranean ones as well, so those of you with heavy feet be warned. If a lot of noise is made on your approach, you will be forewarn-

ing an educated survivor, giving it a chance to find the stop ends and hiding shelves in advance, even before a net has been taken out of the bag. I know it's not possible to be ghostly quiet, but a degree of field craft or common sense is required.

RABBIT DISEASES

Myxomatosis

We should all know about myxomatosis by now, but what I didn't know was that it was down to one man's quest to rid his own land of rabbits that caused our countryside to experience the frequent and sickening sight of rabbits dying from this disease. The situation before this disease struck the UK can only be described as a modernday ferreter's dream *or* nightmare. Large quantities of rabbits were caught for food or as a saleable commodity and, as such, rabbit trapping, snaring, netting and ferreting were big business, especially for unmarked rabbits during and after the war. Just before myxomatosis hit, the stable population was estimated at 60 million rabbits plus, while the estimated rabbit damage in 1950 was £50 million, with its equivalent today being astronomical.

During Britain's rabbit boom, over on the other side of the world Australia deliberately infected its rabbit population (which had increased from the twenty-four wild rabbits introduced by Thomas Austin in 1859 for hunting purposes to an estimated 600 million by 1950) with the deadly virus, myxomatosis. The result was the removal of 90 per cent of Australia's rabbits and a considerable reduction in the catastrophic damage done to the land. Word spread about these results and in Maillebois, northern France, a bacteriologist called Dr Paul Armand Delille had a pair of rabbits inoculated with the myxomatosis virus in a bid to rid his private estate of rabbits. Within a few months, not only had his rabbits gone but also the local population. Soon the national population of rabbits had been seriously reduced and then myxomatosis reached the rest of Europe and North Africa. In 1953, it crossed the channel and hit the UK, the main means of transmission being the mosquito, the midge and the rabbit flea.

The initial point of spread was thought to be via mosquitoes from France. During the warm weather not only fleas but also mosquitoes were attacking the infected rabbits of France. The warm thermals above the French coast sucked the mosquitoes that had been feeding on the infected rabbits up to a height of a few thousand feet and carried them across the sea. Once around the British coastline the cooler air dropped the thermals and the mosquitoes that were now hungry, infected and ready to unleash the virus on the British rabbit population.

By 1955, 99 per cent of the UK's rabbits had perished. Many cursed the sight and smell of the decomposing flesh of the sick and dying animals, but not everyone was sad to see the decline of the rabbit. Landowners in particular welcomed the rapid decline in the rabbit population and to this day many will aim to give the disease a helping hand by moving affected rabbits about on land to try to infect new, stronger animals. The result of the decline was a dramatic improvement in harvests and the outlook of the land changed due to the lack of grazing of certain plants,

Myxomatosis: it was only a matter of time before it hit the UK. (Author)

which allowed everything to grow and spread unhindered.

I have spoken to many eyewitnesses of this disease and the only thing I can add is that I am glad it wasn't introduced in my time. Livelihoods were wiped out at a stroke; no rabbits meant that rabbit catchers were surplus to requirements, with the result that all those years of skill, experience and graft became redundant. It took fifteen years before the rabbit population reached a mere 5 per cent (3 million) of the pre-myxomatosis population and another five years to reach 20 per cent (12 million). Now, more than fifty years later, the population is estimated to be 45 million, which is 75 per cent of the pre-myxomatosis population. The twenty-first century rabbit is once more a major agricultural pest, hence the rebirth of the traditional methods of rabbit catching.

Myxomatosis is a disease caused by the myxoma virus, which affects only the rabbit, both wild and domestic. The virus was discovered originally in South America. It is carried and spread by the flea, tick and mosquito, and, although no official study has confirmed this, midges and gnats are thought to transmit the disease as well. The vectors live on the blood of the animal, then spread it by feeding on another host animal. The flea has the extraordinary capability of surviving for up to six months after the rabbit has left its warren, ready to infect any new residents.

Taking into account the travelling range, including wind assistance, of mosquitoes and midges, this allows a greater area and distance between transmissions of the virus than is usually travelled by the rabbit alone, thus causing the spread of the virus between colonies of rabbits. The mosquito, midge and other blood-feeding creatures are having a greater effect due to the warmer climate and the lack of frosts to kill them off during the winter. With today's greater movement, we can inadvertently spread disease around the country via our clothing, animals and vehicles. In 2007 the myxomatosis outbreak was more widespread due to the amount of stagnant water around after the summer floods and the generally warmer weather.

2007 also saw a first ever-recorded outbreak of bluetongue in the UK, a disease that affects cattle, sheep, goats and deer. Midges of the *Culicoides* group, such as *C.obsoletus*, *C.pulicaris*, *C.dewulfi* and other act as vectors where they occurred across the UK. Although we have had no official study into this subject, if these types of midges can puncture the hide of a cow and spread bluetongue, what is stopping it doing the same to a rabbit and spreading myxomatosis? As we know, the flea and tick are vectors of myxomatosis underground, but as our climate gets warmer, rabbits are spending a lot more time above ground and are still becoming affected by myxomatosis. It seems fair to say that the gnat/midge could be another vector of myxomatosis.

Once infected, it takes around ten to fourteen days for the rabbit's life to end. The disease spreads from the initial point of infection to the lymph nodes, blood and then to the spleen and liver. Within days, all orifices have swelled and a poison puss is emitted, giving the flies a chance to host this animal whilst still alive. Of those rabbits that recover from the disease, the majority are immune to reinfection for the rest of their lives, passing on a passive immunity of short duration to their young. However, due to the short lifespans of rabbits, often little more than a year in the wild, this has little effect in practice. What has been more important is the in-built genetic immunity of certain rabbits in the population. Survival of these rabbits, combined with their high reproduction rate and the death of the competition, meant that a population of myxomatosis-resistant rabbits quickly built up, explaining the rapid rise of the once-decimated rabbit population.

In 2006, we saw the arrival of a mutated strain of myxomatosis, with different opinions as to how it was being transmitted. It appeared stronger, affected more land than ever before and was transported and transmitted by a different vector. It appears that since the initial outbreak, the rabbit has grown a natural resistance to this disease and its mutated forms, to the extent that in 2007, there was an estimated 40 to 50 per cent mortality rate (although based on my own experience, I would say it was more like 30 per cent).

There are several strains of myxomatosis. The strongest strain will kill in roughly fourteen days, while a weaker strain will take between eighteen to twenty-eight days, although a rabbit might survive this weaker strain, passing on a certain amount of immunity to any offspring. However, as the weaker strain is present longer it may infect more fit rabbits than the stronger virus.

Whilst going about my daily jobs, I have often been stopped in my tracks by the sight of an ailing rabbit. I always do the decent thing and relieve the rabbit of its agony, humanely dispatching it to end its suffering. I cannot believe that in some quarters of modern-day Britain, industries are calling for a reintroduction of myxomatosis, thereby condemning infected rabbits to die in a horrific manner, which, if put into human terms, would be completely unacceptable.

The Pests Act of 1954 criminalized intentional transmission of myxomatosis, but it was inevitable that infected rabbits were brought into the UK to spread the disease, as no rabbits meant larger crop yields and more money for the farmers, landowners and growers. However, few were prosecuted due to the difficulty in actually catching the culprit in the act of transmission. The resulting near-extermination of the rabbit raised various political questions, as many found myxomatosis appalling for humanitarian and ethical reasons, while farmers and landowners welcomed the arrival of this virus purely on an economic basis. Animal welfare groups considered the use of the gun, trap, dog, ferret and net to be preferable to control by biological warfare. Hunters, trappers and sportsmen were disgusted by the disease, for not only did it eliminate their quarry, but it also resulted in an unnecessarily lingering death for millions of rabbits.

During the initial outbreak of myxomatosis, MAFF (Ministry of Agriculture, Food and Farming) was alarmed at the prospect of so much readily available food becoming scarce so soon after World War II. A natural by product of the countryside, the rabbit was a pest alive but a family meal dead and for this reason MAFF did everything in its power to halt the unnatural spreading of myxomatosis. Thousands of rabbits were brought into markets such as Smithfield in London to supply the nation with meat, but as we now know, deliveries were soon to be stopped.

Finally, how do we learn from the history and results of myxomatosis in the UK when faced with other animal disease crises in recent years? During the BSE outbreak, foot and mouth and with the emergence of avian influenza and blue tongue around the world, concerns have been raised about certain diseases jumping the species barrier. In the earlier period of the myxomatosis outbreak, some feared that the disease might affect humans. The result was the demise of the rabbit as profitable meat in the decades that followed the initial outbreak, something that we are still affected by today in 2007, when we try to find an outlet for our ferreted rabbits.

Viral Haemorrhagic Disease

Viral Haemorrhagic Disease (VHD) is a deadly disease that any rabbit, wild or domestic, can catch and once infected fatalities are very high. First confirmed in the UK in 1994 in Kent and Devon and although totally different to myxomatosis, it was a notifiable disease until October 1996, when MAFF (now the Department for Environment, Food and Rural Affairs [DEFRA]) lifted restrictions on affected land. The disease had become so widespread across the UK that such measures were useless.

VHD is widespread amongst the British wild rabbit population. When the rabbit catches this disease, the virus heads for the

If there is a positive to be gained from an outbreak of myxomatosis, it is the chance to give a young dog a relatively easy retrieve to hand. (Steven Taylor)

liver, causing massive inflammation and deranged blood clotting, so that internal bleeding then occurs. It has a high mortality rate (90 per cent) and with the speed at which it strikes, no treatment is possible once the rabbit has been infected. However, it is important to note that fatality rates vary from area to area. In some outbreaks in Europe and particularly in the UK, only a small number of rabbits from the infected population died. Baby rabbits under about eight weeks of age typically do not show any signs of illness, but the disease is usually fatal in rabbits over eight weeks. Infected rabbits may die suddenly, with no outward sign of illness, or they may become very ill before dying, experiencing difficulty in breathing, loss of appetite, a high temperature and bleeding from the nose and bottom. A small percent-

age of rabbits develop a more chronic form of the illness and may die of liver failure.

Up to the end of 1996, the South-West, Wales and coastal areas were worst affected, but because the disease is no longer notifiable there is no way of knowing where VHD is currently most active. It is important to note that it is illegal to release VHD or myxomatosis into the wild rabbit population.

Pasteurella Multocida

Unlike the foreign lands across the water, we have always thought of our country as being safe when it comes to diseases we can catch from our native animals. However, with a changing climate and overpopulation of all animals including humans, this now looks likely to change. In 2006, we learned that Pasteurella multocida, or its common name of 'snuffles' or 'rabbit flu', had caused the tragic death of a young farmer. The death was a shock to those of us who hunt rabbits and are therefore in close and frequent contact with them. Over the years, the human hand has accounted for millions of rabbits, but until recently very little has been known about this potentially lethal threat from the rabbit.

'Rabbit flu' is a well-known cause of mortality in rabbits, although the disease is not in fact flu and is caused by a different organism. Pasteurella multocida can be carried by and causes disease worldwide in a range of animals, not just rabbits. The death of the young farmer was the fifth fatality, the other four being between 1993 and 2003, with about 400 laboratory-confirmed cases reported in humans each year in England and Wales. Most of these cases occur in people over fifty years of age. The rabbit and many of our livestock and wildlife carry this disease (although the majority of cases are caught from cats or dogs), but some patients have had no animal contact. The disease can be contracted through dog and cat bites, scratches or licks, especially through an open wound, so always carry some water and suitable handwash or baby wipes to clean up at the end of the day, or before eating/smoking. When ferreting you are always getting scratched by the claws of the rabbit, and by thorns and bushes, especially when clearing or setting nets. In this health and safety obsessed world, I am positive we will soon be told to wear full protective clothing, but just as long as it comes in green.

So what should you do if you have been scratched or bitten by an animal? You should gently clean the area around the bite/scratch and seek medical attention if signs of infection appear, such as redness, pain or swelling. This advice is the same for any animal bite. However, the information made available to me states that if you are in a high-risk group (with a weakened immune system), you should seek medical attention immediately after any animal bite. Will all of this stop anyone going out? Of course not, but what it should do is make us realize that a little hygiene at the end of the day or night might just ensure that we go out for another day.

One factor remains, though, to which most of us who handle affected rabbits probably never give a second thought. When handling rabbits, and especially ones that have just been dispatched, it is important to bear in mind what happens or is happening to the fleas on such animals. Once the rabbit is dead, the host fleas have to find another meal ticket and more often than not they will try to bag a lift from you, your clothes, game bags and especially your car and car carpets, on which your dogs most likely sit. If you are visiting sites on a daily basis that are miles apart, just be aware that you could be inadvertently spreading disease!

CHAPTER THREE

The Ferreter and the Land that is Being Ferreted

It is the ferreter who has the responsibility of ensuring that the ferrets' hard work underground isn't carried out in vain. A true ferreter is someone who not only uses the ferret to control the rabbit population, but also does everything within his power to ensure that the future of ferreting is protected by law and that there is a continuing supply of land on which to ferret, while also maintaining a good stock of ferrets. We must ensure that all aspects of ferreting are openly explained and demonstrated to those who want to continue our fine traditions. Ferreting is about far more than just sending a ferret underground to flush out a rabbit; it is about the bond that unites the ferreter with his animals and the countryside in which they work. It is about the full spectrum of ferret welfare where good working ferrets are healthy ferrets. It is about learning to become part of nature as opposed to being an intruder in it.

When you look at what ferreters do, a sobering image is thrust upon the unaccustomed. The thought of going out in all weather conditions to dig holes and chase rabbits seems absurd. But true ferreters just tuck up their collars and go ferreting. However old you are, when you pass a field full of rabbits you find yourself subconsciously working them, the addictiveness of tackling nature's obstacles treading that fine line between success and failure. We ferret because we enjoy pitting our instincts and skills against those of the rabbit. It is this strong urge to hunt that gets us out in weather that many consider foul. The thought of going ferreting for some ferreters ensures a nervous night's sleep due to the anticipation of the day ahead.

Ferreting doesn't discriminate against colour, religion or sex – anyone can participate with the barest of equipment or the smallest piece of permission. To ensure the continuation of our fine tradition, serious newcomers should be assisted to become involved. Those new to the game should be allowed to make up their own minds about it. Ferreting has no middle ground – people will either love it or loathe it. Ferreting is easily accessible to many different walks of life, to people with different standards, opinions, thoughts and methods. Obviously it is hard for those with any degree of mobility problems as ferreting usually takes place in fields or ditches, but it is not impossible. Only by looking at those who practise ferreting for sport or work, novice to experienced, can we to learn to improve our ways and methods. We must come to appreciate the broad spectrum of methods available. If we take the time to look, listen and not be afraid to admit that no one person has all of the answers, whoever we are or whatever we do, we can all benefit from new learning experiences.

We all have our own style and area of ferreting, which only serves to add to the fascination of ferreting. Each day spent ferreting will be unique, as is each landscape that we ferret. We are all dealing with the unpredictability of nature. All we can do is reduce the avenues of escape, reduce the odds down to our favour and rely on a bit of luck now and again.

It is always sensible to listen to those who have local knowledge of the ferreting ground. (Steven Taylor)

OPPOSITE: Enthusiasm is nothing without opportunity. (Author)

Whether you are ferreting for sport or professionally, the difference to the day will be made by your approach, attitude and pending results. I have puzzled and annoyed many friends by noting the tally of not the ones in the bag but the ones that have escaped. There are always going to be times when you think you have everything covered and then the rabbit has that little bit of luck and manages to escape. Sometimes that one unseen hole will be the one that the rabbit bolts from, or one net will be set slightly wrongly, or, when you take your shot, the rabbit may run behind a tree stump that very second.

If there is one aspect of ferreting that irritates me, it is unduly educating the rabbit; unless I can ferret a spot to my satisfaction, I won't do it. Analysing the reasons for their escape and learning to prevent any further

mistakes is a lesson we all get given from time to time. Admitting that you will not catch everything, no matter how good you think you are, is a vital admission for the ferreter to make. It is a pointless exercise to believe you will go out and catch everything, because I'm afraid the odds are heavily stacked against you.

I am often asked, 'What separates success from failure whilst ferreting?' Apart from Lady Luck, it has to be the psyche of each individual ferreter. Anybody can catch rabbits, but it is when you need to outsmart your quarry and work that bit harder when you least want to which can make the difference. It might require you to position the nets differently or change tactics whilst the ferrets are down if you aren't happy. It is a balance between not losing sight of your plan and overcoming the many problems that ferreting offers.

THE DIFFERENT
TYPES OF FERRETER

There are many different types of ferreter, ranging from the happy-go-lucky ferreter who lays a few nets, catches a few rabbits and doesn't worry if some escape, to the ferreter who goes ferreting without the aid of the ferret finder and happily keeps ferrets that are not accustomed to the hands of the human. You then have the ferreter who, after working hard all week, wants to unwind and relax, bolt a few into the nets or just shoot enough to feed the dogs, ferrets and make up the petrol money. They treat their pastime with a high degree of professionalism and their equipment backs this up. We then have those who own every new gadget and piece of overpriced and ill-designed clothing just because it is in vogue, placing how they look over how they ferret. Then there are those who see themselves as poachers, walking with the barest of kit, so that if they are found out, they can hide/lose their gear and run faster, forgetting about a generally collarless ferret. These ferreters usually convince themselves that they are the last of the great hunters.

A ferreter in the true sense of the word has a mind that is attuned to what he is about to do, irrespective of the time spent in the field, the clothing on his back, or the amount of equipment readily available. The essential pieces of equipment cost nothing financially, as knowledge, commitment and field craft – laying the nets, silently standing in the right position and having the respect to dispatch the bolted rabbit humanely – all combine to make the cornerstone of what we want to achieve. True ferreting is the feeling you get within when everything clicks into place. The difference lies within; there are people who go ferreting, then there are ferreters.

I have worked with many different ferreters, from those who can only go out occasionally due to their work commitments to the professional pest controller. Whatever situation we find ourselves in, we must remember that every time we go ferreting, we don't just represent ourselves but the whole of the ferreting community, aiming to get the right sort of reputation which takes years to build up, but, if you are not careful, only seconds to destroy.

THE CHOICES AND DECISIONS
INVOLVED IN FERRETING

Ferreting is like everything in life, with various choices and decisions to be made. Get these in the right order and the quantity and quality of your ferreting can be very high and rewarding. Get them wrong and you have another of life's experiences hopefully to learn from. By making the right decisions at the right time you can make ferreting look easier than it actually is, but the one guarantee is that there will be problems along the way. The ferreter with the foresight to think ahead, from how many ferrets will be needed to the clothes to be worn, will always reap more rewards. The wrong decision can be uncomfortable to say the least, but the feeling you get when you realize that some vital piece of kit has been left behind is gut-wrenching. Think carefully about where and how long you envisage ferreting in any one particular warren. If the day is not going according to plan, bail out and move on. You are doing no one any favours standing about getting frustrated.

If the rabbits aren't bolting for whatever reason and you can move on, do so, for your time is a precious commodity. Unless you have to, why stay in warrens that openly invite digging? Enjoy yourself, clear up some rabbits and cover as much ground as your day allows. The ferreter who continually works the sticky spots is usually the one who gets paid for doing so. When you only have the weekend in which to ferret you have no choice other than to go out or stay in, but it helps to ferret in acceptable weather; the rabbits will still be there a week later. Those who ferret all week have little option other than switching a day or two in case of extreme weather, because if a job is put back too many times it gives the rabbit a chance to spread and move on to a greater area than you first envisaged ferreting.

Before entering the ferrets, it always pays to check out the immediate surroundings for any missing bolt-holes. (Steven Taylor)

The rabbit must be dispatched quickly, humanely and efficiently at all times. (Steven Taylor)

OPPOSITE: *A ferreter in the true sense of the word is focused on what he is about to do. (Steven Taylor)*

RESPECT AND ATTITUDE

One of the most essential yet fast-disappearing values of modern-day society is respect. Respecting your quarry, equipment or ground is, to me, second nature, for if you lack respect, how can you expect others to respect you? We have the luxury of looking into the harsh reality of the past from our ivory towers; though we all have our hardships, they do not compare with the poverty of years ago, when the rabbit was truly a valuable commodity that demanded the respect of its pursuers. To me, respect means essentially simple things such as getting permission to ferret, using a ferret finder to ensure that the ferret goes home with you and ensuring that no cruelty is inadvertently handed out to the rabbit and every dispatch is carried out as humanely and efficiently as possible. Clearing up any mess after you, be it filling in holes you have dug or not leaving litter, and avoiding where you have been told not to go are all forms of respect that should be automatic. By respecting our environment we ensure that it is kept in order. If we don't, then our job will be made much harder, as some of us are now experiencing.

The conduct of each and every ferreter doesn't just reflect on that particular individual – it reflects on the whole of ferreting and, more importantly, on those who wish to continue long after an individual may have packed in ferreting. Although it appears large, we in fact live in a very small world and pictures showing controversial aspects of our way of life will do us no favours among those who wish to curtail our daily activities. We must all learn to look at the bigger picture, as the days of just going out ferreting have long gone. We must be the diplomat, politician, environmentalist and so on if we are to educate the wider world to understand what vital work we carry out, for both their and our benefit.

FIELD CRAFT

This is the most important aspect of ferreting in my opinion, but one that is disappearing at a rate of knots. This piece of equipment will cost you nothing in financial terms, but can cost you a lot of rabbits if not mastered and used accordingly. More often than not, it is field craft that separates the hunter/gatherer/provider/conservationist from someone just out for a spot of ferreting.

Field craft provides you with a vital insight into nature. It enables you to plan your forays, become a part of nature and the surrounding countryside and ensures that you think like any other predator. It enables you to read the signals that the weather, animals and countryside present to us. The biggest lovers of the countryside are those who understand how it works and, more importantly, why. True conservation involves the jobs of pest and predator control in order to stop certain species from becoming overpopulated and therefore affecting the population of other species, be it flower, bird or mammal. It is only when you spend a large amount of time engulfed in a certain environment that you learn to appreciate its ways and requirements. You must then learn to counteract successfully any obstacle in your way. This makes field craft an essential ingredient to any ferreter.

Alertness, steadiness, patience and having an understanding of the situation, along with silence, are essential. However, in certain environments it is impossible to keep silent. If you cannot visibly see each other you need sound to communicate. Many people ferret big, thick hedgerows, bushes or buildings, making a degree of noise inevitable. It then becomes a matter of knowing when to speak and move and when not to. There should be no chatting, smoking or stamping your feet to keep warm. These actions may be taken for granted by the masses, but the ferreter must keep all unnecessary disturbance to a minimum. Allowable movement is when net setting amongst hedgerows requires last-minute clearances, in order for the nets to work properly and not get snagged by any twigs or undergrowth.

When you understand how nature works, you start to realize how unpredictable things can be. Contrary to what has been said above, very noisy days can sometimes be more productive than completely silent ones. We all continue to learn and gain knowledge and experience from our times in the fields, which is why no two days are the same and field craft cannot be taught sat at home in front of a screen.

WHEN DOES SPORT BECOME CONTROL AND VICE VERSA?

However, wherever or whenever you go ferreting, it can be pigeonholed into two different types, ferreting for pest control or sporting purposes. I have practised both forms and have found that how the day is perceived and the seriousness in which the ferreting is practised separate the business from a bit of

Field craft is taught, not bought. (Steven Taylor)

The image of an old man, a ferret and a few nets has outstayed its welcome; enter the new age of ferreting. (Greg Knight)

sport. Ferreting as a method of pest control when practised competently is continuing to become an efficient and cost-effective alternative to gassing, as not every rabbit hole can be legally gassed.

Ferreting for pest-control purposes is a world away from the popular perception that all ferreting is carried out with a single ferret and a handful of nets. Professional ferreting occurs within a pressurized environment built upon expected results, as the customer usually expects a large reduction in the population of rabbits. This ensures a rush of adrenalin when everything falls into place, but creates frustration and disappointment when it doesn't. We all know how unpredictable the weather can be and how outside influences such as stock, people and so on can influence the day, with the result that the expected

OPPOSITE: Ferreting, when practised competently, is an efficient alternative to gassing, as not every rabbit warren can be legally gassed. (Steven Taylor)

results do not always materialize and, along with them, the possibilities of further contracts.

There are certain differences in mindset between the professional and sporting ferreter. To the former, a rabbit becomes a rabbit, no matter what size, shape, colour or age it is, whereas a sportsman doesn't want to do himself out of rabbits for next year's ferreting. Control consists of looking at the rabbit as work and not as quarry to be held in awe. We all respect the rabbit, but when controlling rabbits for a profession, the pregnant doe isn't left behind to raise a litter then breed again and young rabbits aren't left behind to eat more of the farmer's valuable crop. At the end of the day, they are all rabbits.

Sporting ferreters will always leave some rabbits for next year or will raise a smile to the escapees. I know rabbits escape and some are left behind, but the professional ferreter should count the rabbits that escape, not the ones in the bag. As previously mentioned, I

Some of the best days I have had ferreting have been when we have a few hours out and then go to the pub for a pint and a bit of grub. (Steven Taylor)

dislike a lot of unnecessary education of the rabbit. Looking at the reasons for the escape, analysing why it happened and learning from your mistakes should reduce the chances of a repeat performance. Was it you, your nets, dog or gun at fault, or was it just a lucky rabbit?

The places that are ferreted differ markedly. Some are worked from necessity, others from choice. Once the paying customer has employed you to control a rabbit problem, even if it is the biggest, most inhospitable warren you have ever seen, that is where you ferret. The ferreter who ferrets for sport will mostly opt for the easy warrens with little undergrowth and fewer holes, whereas for control, the difficult warrens are ferreted early on and then the smaller ones left for later on in the day. The attitude and the effect on the atmosphere

are different too. During work, the atmosphere is silent, with an attitude that is as professional as any other tradesman at work and in this way you can fully concentrate on the job in hand.

When ferreting large areas, the warrens that are ferreted first are then backfilled. This involves filling in all of the entrances and exits with the surrounding soil, to completely block the holes. The smaller warrens should be quicker to ferret in the time allowed at the end of the day. Backfilling is done both to show the customer that a particular area has been ferreted and also for the ferreter to check whether any rabbits have returned or escaped. When ferreting the next warren, escapees sometimes head for the previous warren, but if it has been backfilled you have shut the door on this particular sanctuary. A good dog or gun will soon put these escapees in the bag. For control purposes, good results can be obtained from ferreting, especially when used in conjunction with other methods of control such as the rifle, trap or net. It is a shame that many farmers or landowners cannot see past their indiscriminate chemical option when it comes to rabbit control, although increasingly they are experiencing the difference and are switching to the more traditional and environmentally friendly option.

I now find that when I go out for a day's ferreting for sport with friends, the expectations have been removed, so the mood is a lot more relaxed and jovial. The ferrets will still work the same, but you don't put the same emphasis on the catch or the time spent ferreting. Some of the best days I have had ferreting have been when we have a few hours out and then go to the pub for a pint and a bit of grub. At the end of the day, we have the rabbits, have enjoyed ourselves and we go home happy.

THE RIGOURS OF A HARD SEASON AND INJURIES

However you ferret, at times it can be hard work. Whether it is digging holes, breaking through tough roots, lifting a heavy bag of rabbits, or creeping about in a hedge bottom, it can all take its toll. We usually ferret when it is cold, with the result that your body is cold when performing all these tasks. Cold muscles and sudden movement can mean a whole range of injuries. Over the course of a year, it can be surprising just how many injuries are picked up whilst ferreting. Probably the most obvious is the bad back, often when the spade is about to be deployed. Nothing brings on a bad back quicker than when asking someone to dig a hole for you! Further risks are twisting your ankles by tripping over unseen rabbit holes, straining tendons in the fingers when grabbing rabbits' back legs whilst digging, or suffering cuts and abrasions from the hidden dangers buried beneath the surface, such

as glass, flint and metal. It is always wise to always carry some form of first-aid kit and eyewash. You will be exposed to the dangers that thorny bushes, trees and fences present. The amount of nicks, cuts and tears received from such obstacles are more commonplace than people take notice of. The most serious accidents are often dealt to cold fingers by a sharp knife, so be careful. It is wise to always be up-to-date with your tetanus injections, and to treat any ailments as soon as you clean up at the end of the day.

FERRETING PARTNERS

If you usually ferret solo, there may come a time when you need some help ferreting a problematic warren, or, if you already have help, you may need an extra pair of hands for those bigger areas. The qualities of a ferreting partner are exactly the same whether canine or human. Ferreting can be intense at times, relaxed at others, so a mixture of skills is required. The traits that I look for in potential partners are that they are honest, trustworthy, keen, reliable and work with a degree of incentive. They should have the honesty to replace everything where it came from and should be trusted not to go back to your permission on their own. They need to be reliable enough to get up on time, whatever the weather. The pair of you need to be able to 'agree to disagree' if necessary, ending the day still as friends. It is always easier to teach good habits to those who are willing to learn rather than trying to correct bad ones in those who aren't. The future of ferreting is in our own hands, so we bear the responsibility for ensuring that anyone young or old who is willing and able to further this traditional country art is given the chance that we were given.

THE TERRAIN WE FERRET

It is a fair assumption to say that every area of the UK has its good and bad spots in which to ferret. By looking at the UK as a whole, you will find that some areas have denser populations of rabbits than others, in the main because they are large uninhabited tracts of land. If the rabbit is left undisturbed by the presence of man, it is also left uneducated about his ways and the threat he poses to the rabbit's existence. This often dictates how individuals operate up and down the country. The local ferreters adapt to the surroundings and if this means that they mooch, hunt or rake about for fewer rabbits, then that is what they do.

The forces of nature have shaped our land into a diverse and rich island where many plants and animals survive and prosper. Because of this diversity, the way in which we ferret is totally reliant upon our local geographical make-up. The United Kingdom is a collection of mountains, hills and lowlands made up of rock, slate, sandstone, limestone and various forms of sand and clay. This substrate dictates how the rabbit builds its home; for example, some warrens are only 12in (30cm) deep because of the underlying rock, or they may be 30ft (9m) deep in sand. Some areas have no or little foliage acting as harbourage against predators, while others are full of thick hedges and woodland.

Hills are scattered throughout the United Kingdom, these being halfway between mountains and lowlands, shading each other and offering rich grazing on the grasslands. The hills formed by a long ridge of limestone and sandstone that stretches from the North Yorkshire moors through the Cotswolds to Lyme Bay in Dorset contain most of Britain's iron ore and some of Britain's finest building stones. The chalky terrain of Sussex also offers a safe home for the rabbit as few holes are dug, but the ancient subterranean piping can

All ferreting partnership will disagree at times but it is important that, at the end of the day, ferreters remain friends. (Steven Taylor)

Geology has shaped our land into a diverse and rich island where many plants and animals survive and prosper. (Author)

be substantial. Ancient large warrens can be seen on land all over the downs, the result of hundreds of years of excavations.

When ferreting on the hills and moors, the warrens are either set in the cracks of rocks or in peaty earth lying on top of rock. Some of these areas may appear to be easier to bolt rabbits, but as any ferreter will tell you, the easiest rabbit in the world is the one that has just been caught. Underneath these rocky masses is an area that cannot easily be penetrated by the spade. Some will ferret these areas but many don't, as a lot of ferrets are lost down natural shafts on such outings.

The lowlands form the remainder of the land. On a map of the United Kingdom, a line could be drawn from the mouth of the Tees in Cleveland to the mouth of the Exe in Devon, with the areas to the east and south of this line being the lowlands. They are flat in some areas, undulating in others, but only a few places rise more than a few hundred feet above sea level. This land signifies the type of countryside regarded by many as being idyllic, that perfect patchwork of fields and hedges. The underlying rock is soft, which in turn produces the rich fertile soils and good grazing land for cattle. Here, the rabbit inhabits many hedgerows as the protection offered by the hedges is far greater than living in a warren on open land, which does not provide the safety of cover from predators.

Historically, when the sea receded, limestone, chalk, clay, gravel and sand were deposited.

Roadside rabbits are often the most difficult to deal with. Note the raised long net to avoid the caught rabbit veering into the road. (Author)

BELOW: *The rabbit will set up home in the safest yet most unlikely of habitats. (Author)*

The sand and clay at the top of the folds were eroded away, remaining only in the Hampshire basin, the Thames Valley, Essex and the coast of East Anglia. In these areas, the warrens are found in all sorts of substrates from the thick clay inland to sandier soils nearer the coast. Unpredictable substrates mean that versatility is required when digging and in the type of digging tool used.

With the changes in the world's climate, the sea is reclaiming many coastal areas. The coastal cliffs are eroding yearly and many marshes that have in the past been reclaimed from the sea are now being reused as flood plains. The rabbit is being forced to move and adapt to strange surroundings and many are living above ground in thick, dense undergrowth as a result, until they are forced underground by predator or weather.

In some locations, the rabbit is exploiting the safety offered by many unusual settings. Rabbit warrens can now be seen on roundabouts, under buildings and especially on roadsides. Roadside rabbits and those on railway property are often the most annoying and problematic rabbits you will experience. These warrens are ferretable *if* the land that you have permission on joins an A, B or C classified road, unlike the warrens alongside motorways. If you want to ferret alongside roads, I would strongly recommend taking some advice from the police over the legal position should a rabbit bolt and cause a car to swerve or have an accident. I have ferreted a fair bit by the side of roads and usually find that with a polite road sign and a long net completely surrounding the area, rabbits behave themselves. The problem nowadays with so many young rabbits about, is that it wouldn't take much for one to squeeze through a net and bolt into the road. You must therefore ask yourself whether it is worth the risk.

At the time of writing, the population of the UK is 61 million, having increased by 20 million since 1901, 10 million since 1951 and 4 million since 1998. The rise in population and growth in urban areas has directly affected how our wildlife lives. Rural land accounts for nearly 90 per cent of the British Isles and two-thirds of it is improved farmland or forest and heath land that is managed. The remaining third is unmanaged land. The urban area only occupies around 8 per cent of the land's area, but this accounts for 80 per cent of the population and industrial sites.

When we take into account the population increase over the decades, we can see that the urban area has encroached onto the rural. This is not just physically with houses, roads and industrial sites, but with an influx of people who often bring very little, if anything, to the community. The countryside now has to cope with an influx of commuters and leisure walkers, all bringing additional pressures to bear on the original occupants, the animals and all those who work and manage the land. The increase in noise and light pollution is often underestimated until you want to go somewhere quiet or out on a dark night with some nets or a dog for a shine (lamping).

There are now more people struggling to hunt whatever quarry they can on less land. It is little wonder that in certain areas the culture is to turn to poaching to fulfil this need to hunt. The local wildlife must feel like it is being hunted on a shift system, with the result that education comes quickly to these animals as there would appear to be no let up in their plight for survival. Fortunately, I have never lived in such an area and so my eyes are firmly on the job in hand rather than constantly looking over my shoulder.

In many ways, it is no longer credible to talk of an urban/rural divide, as a large proportion of people who practise country pursuits can no longer afford to live in the countryside. The housing market in rural areas is being swamped by those who can afford the high prices, but unfortunately in many cases these newcomers have no desire to adapt to their rural surroundings. They are often ignorant of country ways and as a result communities are starting to break down. The new rural dwellers look the part only when it suits them, but when the muck gets spread, the hunt passes through, or cockerels start crowing at 4am it is a totally different story. I know many a countryman, woman and child who has been raised in an urban environment – the passion, knowledge and pride for the countryside is within the person, not the postcode.

With the lack of consistently cold winters, insects that are usually killed off, such as the fly, are in abundance.

THE CHANGING WEATHER

Over the years, we have been fed a romantic rustic image of a cold frosty morning being the perfect weather for ferreting. But is there such a thing as the perfect ferreting weather? On average, the weather will play little part in the rabbit's decision to vacate its home. If the rabbit wants to come out, it will do so, irrespective of what the weather is doing. In fact, a frosty morning often provides the worst conditions in which to ferret. If a rabbit is alarmed when feeding in the field, it will stamp its feet in warning and the frozen ground will carry this sound further than softer soil would. In addition, it is more difficult to get pegs and poles into solid ground, not to mention how much harder the digging is. But in fact frost is no longer the most common type of winter weather, at least in the more southerly parts of the UK, where the milder winters have seen a great increase in rainfall in the winter months.

In September, the weather used to change, frosts and snow were commonplace and the amount of rainfall was only a fraction of what we presently experience. Nowadays, we can have flyblown rabbits in the middle of winter due to the fact that the weather isn't cold enough to kill off the flies, as would have been the case a decade ago. But we have to move with the times and our surroundings. The worst weather for ferreting is often heavy wind and rain, but, as I have experienced, if rabbits want to come out, they will. I like ferreting in the snow, though this is fairly rare nowadays. The fresh snow conceals as much activity as it highlights. Inactive holes are therefore covered in snow, but recently laid tracks and active holes are clearly seen. One way of spotting an occupied warren in deep frosts or light snow is to inspect the surrounding edges of the entrance/exit holes, which may be rimed by melting snow or ice. Alternatively, you may see the visible signs of the rabbit's breath against the colder atmosphere.

Because the weather patterns are changing over time, our land has adapted and for many

The warm air from the inhabited warren melts the ice and snow around the holes. (Author)

plants and animals the change seems to be for the better. If nature can adapt, why do so many of us find it difficult to move away from the familiarity that tradition brings? We seem to have a preconditioned outlook when it comes to what weather suits ferreting best. We have to be as adaptable as possible to ensure we make the most out of all weather conditions. Of course, I know that in some extreme conditions ferreting is pointless, but if you want to be out or have booked in a certain job on a certain day, then you are out ferreting, plain and simple. I have ferreted in every weather condition imaginable, from gales to driving rain to snow blizzards. Undoubtedly, I believe that the rabbit doesn't like some weather conditions like high winds and torrential rain, but on the whole I think

the ferreter worries about the weather more than the animals that have to live with it. As time goes on, I find that the human tolerance for persevering in harsh weather conditions is diminishing.

We are continually reading about and experiencing the change in our climate. This climate change is being experienced globally. Over the last 1,000 years the warmest century was the last, the twentieth century, with the 1990s being the warmest decade in the last one hundred years. The results of a warmer climate are the change in rainfall patterns and the rise in sea levels as the ice caps melts. Extreme weather patterns are on the increase. When we talk about the climate, we refer to the average weather experienced over a long period, typically thirty

A white or light-coloured ferret is more easily spotted above ground. (Greg Knight)

years. This includes the temperature, rainfall and wind patterns.

The resulting changes in our climate mean that the average temperature in the UK will become warmer on the land and slightly lower in the water. The summers will be warmer, while the sharp winters of old will become a rarity. The winters will become warmer, with an increase in rainfall and decrease in snowfall. Today, we are likely to experience practically all of the weather patterns within any season; some days in the winter it can be as warm as the summer, while some days in the summer, it can be as cold as in winter.

With the rise in average temperature, the growing season has been extended and heatwaves during the summer decrease the likelihood of frost and snow in the winter. The loss of the colder weather ensures that the undergrowth and foliage are high and green for longer as each year passes. The winters have become wetter, with the majority of the winter rain and snow falling in shorter bursts, delivering more inches overall than fifty years ago.

The rabbit does not have a calendar to say what month it is, so when and where we go ferreting is dictated to us by the changing weather and seasons. We can no longer count on the frost to kill off the undergrowth, so that it is now constantly growing, with the nettles still stinging and as high as ever. This increase in foliage means that the possibility of missing holes, never mind the cleverly camouflaged bolt-holes, is greater than ever before. To counteract this sea of green and brown cover, a large percentage of modern-day ferreters are now advocating the use of white or light-coloured ferrets, simply because they can be more easily spotted.

OPPOSITE: *Because we experience snow less frequently than we did, out tolerance to its harshness has diminished. (Author)*

CHAPTER FOUR

The Ferreter's Equipment

The whole point of ferreting is to catch the fleeing rabbit, therefore it is the ferreter's job to decide which method to utilize in order to achieve this. There are several options available, consisting of the net, dog, gun and hawk, either singly or in combination. The common denominator to all these methods is that the ferret is used to persuade the rabbit to bolt from its warren. Underneath the ground, the mechanics are exactly the same, as the ferret's ability to work isn't dictated by what method you are using above ground. The ferret simply pleases its own instinct to hunt. Above the warren, the ferreter must think hard and logically about what he wants to achieve and construct a plan of action.

A bolted rabbit has the ability to make the best of dogs look silly at times. (Steven Taylor)

OPPOSITE: *The fixed net method of long netting has improved many ferreters' quality of ferreting and quantity of rabbits. (Steven Taylor)*

Are you going to ferret in the true sense of the word with nets, or are you going out to bolt a few rabbits to give a hawk a flight or two, or to watch as a dog pursues the fleeing rabbit in a bid to catch and retrieve it back to its handler? I believe that true ferreting is with nets because the focus is entirely on the ferret's ability to work. When using a bird or a dog, the focus is more on the pursuit of the rabbit once it has been bolted than on the actual bolt itself. The aim of the vast majority of ferreters is to control rabbits, hence their use of a combination of nets, guns and dogs. In this way, when two or three rabbits bolt at the same time, the escape routes should have been covered.

To go ferreting, the equipment needed can be as basic or as complicated as you want to make it. With the expansion of the modern media, we read and hear so many more opinions and examples of equipment that are toted as the 'new wheel'. One of the distractions given to us today is our weakness for trends. Your judgement may be clouded by the fancy new gear, whether you need it or not; many buy it simply because they can. I truly believe that apart from the materials we use, and of course this also means electronics, do we really need anything different to what was used twenty or more years ago? The old hands caught much more game with half of the equipment we use and I feel we should return to some of these methods, using good old-fashioned field craft and patience. If in the end your equipment hinders rather than helps you, it is not equipment but just plain junk.

GAINING PERMISSION AND HOW TO KEEP IT

Gaining permission is one of the aspects of ferreting that has a lot to do with luck. Irrespective of your location, if you are in the right place at the right time you will strike lucky and get some cracking land to ferret. If you live in an area where a lot of people go ferreting, you will find it harder to gain sole, or

any, permission than if you live where hardly anyone ferrets. The harsh reality, though, is that some shady characters have stung landowners and farmers and we all then pay the price for the loss of trust. You must be able to persuade the person in charge of the land that you are after rabbits and rabbits only, not birds, hares or anything else that you come across. Trust plays a big part in gaining and keeping permission. The land you want to go on is essentially somebody's home and the last thing they want is strangers coming onto the land and helping themselves to whatever they want. You need to be able to put your case forward in a sensible, professional manner, thinking ahead to all those awkward questions you may be asked and showing that some thought has gone into why you are there.

One of the most annoying aspects of trying to gain permission is the frustration experienced when approaching land that is riddled with rabbits, but the landowner, farmer or keeper will not let anyone on to ferret it. This is particularly annoying if the landowner has experienced the support of the ferreting community with regard to the political issues now facing the countryside but is not prepared to return the favour. The land on which I have permission has keepers and they advise when and where to go and their decision is final. If I have to wait until the end of the season, the rabbits are usually in young and unwilling to bolt, so ferreting is therefore made harder and the shoot will have missed an opportunity to get rid of more rabbits than they could have done.

Show whoever you are seeking out that you are reliable, trustworthy and have thought about what you are asking. If you are a newcomer, try the local ferreters to see if one would act as a mentor. Join one of the many country pursuit organisations and ask their local representatives if they have any contacts. Insurance is required in whatever we do nowadays and by being a member of an organization you will automatically be covered by their insurance.

When you do approach the subject of permission, I have always found that the personal touch is better than a letter, phone call or e-mail, although it is important to consider the first impression you will give and to present yourself accordingly. Put yourself in the shoes of the farmer. If you see a smartly dressed person approaching you, you will be far more at ease than if faced by someone scruffy. This may be unfair, but it is a fact of life. Point out to the farmer the advantages of having an extra pair of eyes looking over the land and that you will be removing rabbits that are costing him money. Offer your services to help beat on one of their shoots; even if this is turned down you will have had the courtesy to offer. Permission is sometimes shared, so a third party will be involved. This can be a good thing, but be wary as another party may blame you if anything goes wrong. Ensure that all parties involved know who is and isn't about at any particular time. It is your reputation at risk; it only takes seconds to destroy a reputation that it may have taken you years to build up. It is always better to be safe than sorry, so permission is best granted in a letter, especially if you work alongside a dog. The Hunting Act 2004 states that the rabbit can be legally hunted, but only if you have permission to hunt it.

Once you have permission, you will need to work to keep it. Do not take on too much land; it is important to ensure that you have adequate time to do a good job and don't just skirt around the area. Ferreting is normally finished by March, but because of the changing climate the land will require some sort of control over the summer. By showing your face during these months with a rifle, net or ferret to hand, you are at least showing the farmer that you are sensible in your outlook. A lot of permission is lost by those ferreters who start October, finish February, then forget about rabbits until the following October. If you are not prepared to give something back to someone who has been good enough to let you on their property, your permission may be lost to someone else who will.

THE FERRET

You don't have to be brain of Britain to work out that in order to go ferreting, you require ferrets! The ferret has been looked at in detail in Chapter 1, but in order to make up your equipment you must consider carefully how many ferrets you will need for the day ahead. Pick more than enough for the day's ferreting in order to give some time for a rest, as an overworked ferret will obviously be less efficient and less productive.

THE ROLE OF THE FERRETER'S DOG

To be successful at ferreting it is essential to be able to distinguish the tell-tale signs of occupancy, whether the rabbits are in the ground, halfway up a dead tree stump or under a building. Nothing frustrates the ferreter more than netting up warrens surrounded by

To avoid working tired ferrets, spread the workload around the team. (Steven Taylor)

I have never met a human that is as adept at marking a rabbit as a good dog. (Nigel Housden / Pinsharp Photography)

evidence pointing towards habitation, just to find out half an hour later that the earth is dry of rabbits. It is human nature to start questioning the ferrets' working ability, but after entering that old trusted jill that *always* bolts rabbits, you accept defeat and realize that the warren is empty. Alternatively, after a windy night what is in fact a well-used warren might be overlooked because it is full of leaves and so looks inactive, but hiding beneath the surface may be half a dozen or so rabbits yet to surface to feed. Another frustrating situation is not having the capability to reach the netted rabbit quickly enough in order to stop it wriggling free or being able to prevent another bolting out of an un-netted hole. To counteract these scenarios, the ferreter may use the services of another ally, the dog.

Never before in ferreting history have we gone through such a period when so many people are utilizing the services of a good dog whilst ferreting. This is another choice you have to make, but when you weigh up the advantages against the disadvantages, you will discover why so many dogs are being trained to go ferreting.

Does one really need a dog to go ferreting? The difference between ferreting with or without a dog can only be answered by each individual ferreter. Some see them as essential; some would like one but haven't the room or time; and some simply don't see the point of taking a dog ferreting. We may not necessarily agree with everybody's opinion on this subject, but we must respect both sides of the argument.

To look at this subject without prejudice, the role of the ferreting dog must be observed closely. A ferreting dog is very different to a dog that simply goes ferreting. The ferreting dog is like any other type of dog used for a pursuit, sport or job which is bred specifically to fulfil a particular task proficiently and professionally, for example the spaniel or labrador for the shooting field, the rottweiler or alsatian for guarding duties, or, in our case, the lurcher for ferreting.

I say lurcher because a high percentage of ferreting dogs are lurchers, although some are terriers, spaniels or just plain mongrels. I am not going to become embroiled here in the age-old argument of what cross or type does this or that better than another, but what I will do is describe a dog I like to take ferreting and the tasks it has to master. It will then be up to you decide whether you need a dog for your ferreting and what type is likely to

suit you best. There are many qualified people around and many books on the subject of working and sporting dogs from which you can obtain in-depth information.

If the question 'What makes a ferreting dog different to a dog that goes ferreting?' were to be posed to the nation's ferreters, you would most likely receive as many different answers as there are ferreters. The fundamental differences that separate ferreters must be borne in mind. As ferreters, hunters, moochers, or whatever you like to call yourself, we all live different lives in different societies and hunt different terrains, so no two people or their land are the same. The reply to the question of an ideal dog for ferreting would therefore be as varied as the land that makes up our island.

At first glance, you could be mistaken for thinking that there isn't a specialist dog bred for the job of ferreting. When you look at the

The ferreting dog is really a luxury that many of us feel we can't do without. (Greg Knight)

When it comes to all-round athleticism, a lurcher is hard to beat. (Steven Taylor)

tasks it has to master you begin to appreciate why you never see one for sale in the classified section of the sporting press. If there were a pedigree dog good enough for this job, foreign or native, they would have been utilized by now. Instead, we generally use a type of dog that is a collection of all the good bits from several different breeds that have been added together to create a lurcher. Although there are many good terriers used for ferreting, they have a number of negatives that have persuaded me not to use them. The terrier has short legs, so although it may be small enough to creep into dense undergrowth, it cannot compare with the longer-legged lurcher when it comes to running. In addition, a ferreting dog needs to be obedient and possess the ability to keep quiet, another two factors that let the majority of terriers down, at least in my experience.

With a good few years of ferreting under my belt, and having experienced both good days and those that have left a sour taste in the mouth, I can honestly say that personal experience has been a fantastic tutor. I can remember in my youth the anticipation of the

arrival of my *Shooting News*, reading the many articles and learning from those who had experienced a life revolving around the rabbit. However, after a couple of decades of my own in the field, one valuable piece of advice I have gleaned is that what works in one situation and for one person, won't necessarily work for another. One of the most painful of lessons I learnt in my youth was the difference between ferreting with and without the assistance of a good dog. Originally, I went ferreting without the aid of a dog. At that time I thought nothing of it, until I started to go ferreting with someone who used a dog, then the penny dropped. Trip after trip, without the dog I ferreted warrens where the farmer had seen most activity, but kept finding nothing, so I thought I must be doing something drastically wrong. The difference was, and still is, a way of finding which warrens are inhabited, and for this a guide is needed. The most important role of the ferreting dog is to act as that guide and to mark inhabited warrens.

All dogs will mark to a fashion, but it is how we read those signals sent out by the dog and how we act on them that will cement in the

Young rabbits may be able to slip through a net, but rarely get past a competent dog. (Greg Knight)

dog's mind the difference between true and false marking. It is essential to ensure that the dog realizes it is no coincidence that when it marks a hole, a ferret is entered and a rabbit exits. Dogs may mark by raising a leg, wagging their tail, or by a slight movement of their head to the side. Whatever you do, though, do not let your dog get into the habit of marking with its head stuck down a hole, snorting heavily, resulting in the whole warren and possibly area knowing that there is danger on the surface. Be prudent with your praise and let the dog know it has performed correctly only when rabbits have emerged from the ground. This will avoid the dog marking any hole in order to receive praise from you. It is also vitally important that the dog should

become accustomed to standing out of sight of the exiting rabbits, otherwise they will go back down to safety and getting them to bolt again will most likely require digging.

The temperament of a dog is sometimes overlooked, as people want drive, brains and an aesthetically pleasing animal to parade around with, but a dog without a good temperament is, in my opinion, nothing more than a liability. The socialization of a dog is very important. It needs to become accustomed to all situations which may, or may not, arise during the twelve months of the year, from being around different animals and livestock to ferreting inside a keeper's release pen (where his pheasants are kept) or a similar poultry house. No one knows the character

71

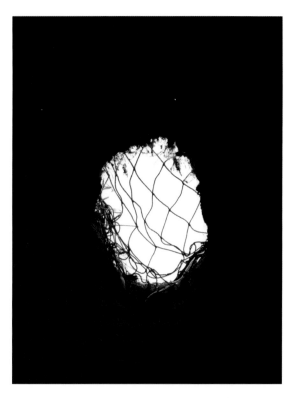

It is important to keep all humans and dogs out of the direct view of the rabbit. (Steven Taylor)

and temperament of your dog better than you do. Creating a strong bond is essential, as you could have the best dog in the world but if you don't get on with it, looking after and living with it day in and day out will be hell. A few times I have seen some fantastic ferreting dogs, but they were unsocialized, solitary workers and defensively aggressive towards any strangers who ventured too close. This isn't a trait I would want in any of my dogs. What I prefer to have around is a relaxed and laid-back dog which is, when required, a little grafter. Ferreting is full of contradictions, so you must ensure that obedience is at an acceptable level before you seriously start the dog out in the field. It goes without saying that a dog that does not follow instructions has no place in the field. The many hours perfecting the retrieve, sit, stay and all the other basic requirements will be tested once real, live game is introduced.

Getting the dog into the field and used to the atmosphere is only the beginning. The dog still has to adapt to the array of equipment that may be in use. The modern preference for using long nets instead of, or in conjunction with, purse nets dictates that any dog, for its own safety, must be aware of the potential dangers of such netting. The long net or purse net is going to stop instantly what the dog would like to chase in full flight, the bolting rabbit. It is therefore the natural reaction of the dog to snatch or grab the bolted rabbit in the net, but it must learn to differentiate between a rabbit caught firmly in a net, a rabbit about to struggle free out of a net and a free-running rabbit.

The long net will pose a few problems for the dog at the start of its training and unless these problems are rectified and mastered, your dog could be laid up with an avoidable injury at a vital time of your ferreting season. The dog's initial reaction is to chase the rabbit and once the rabbit becomes caught in the long net, the dog will follow, especially if using a dark net that easily blends into its surroundings. If you have sensibly acclimatized your dog to the long net, it should jump over or back off from the netted rabbit. However, even after some dogs have been given plenty of opportunity to see what a long net is, training, playing or working around it, they are just not capable of grasping what is required of them. For a dog to run into the net continually, it is not only dangerous to itself, but also costly to the ferreter, as the net will require regular repair. Ears, dew claws and feet can be severely damaged by the twine of a net, acting like a cheese cutter to any animal hitting it at speed.

The most instinctive way to teach a dog about netting is to let it see the nets as often as you can and the dog will present to you its natural way of dealing with a netted rabbit. A lot of dogs chase the rabbit into the net, jump over the net and hold the rabbit. Some

OPPOSITE: Obedience is the cornerstone of the ferreting dog. (Steven Taylor)

Teaching a young dog to respect the rabbit, even after it has bitten a hole in the long net. (Steven Taylor)

BELOW: *The young dog is holding onto a rabbit that has gone through the meshes of this 6z long net. (Steven Taylor)*

The dog can reach a purse net a lot quicker than most ferreters. (Greg Knight)

do this from the back, some from the front, whereas others will make a lunge for the rabbit and become embroiled in the net itself. The most logical stance would be to stand in front of the net, staring at the caught rabbit until the ferreter can dispatch and release the rabbit from the grasp of the net. Keep the dog on a training lead during the first few outings and calmly walk it up to the netted rabbit, teaching it to stand off and at the front of the net. By doing so, if the rabbit was to move, it would try to move away from the dog and deeper into the netting, whereas if the dog was at the back of the net, the rabbit may push forwards and inadvertently release itself. Although a confusing time for an inexperienced dog, and one which will require time and patience from you, once the dog has gained experience it will instinctively decide when it should or shouldn't hold a netted rabbit.

The requirements of each different region will dictate how and where each net is set.

The majority are used to surround bushes that can't be netted and open warrens, or are used as small stop nets pushed through hedging. They can be combined with the purse or poke net to gain maximum efficiency. Wherever you are setting your long nets, ensure that the dog knows where they are, as some nets are unnoticeable against the background, even to a dog used to nets. If the dog doesn't know where they are and is chasing a rabbit through thick undergrowth or hedging, the likelihood is that the dog will become netted too.

Where purse nets are concerned, a dog can reach them a lot quicker than any human, especially up and down ditches or on vast open warrens. It is imperative that the dog becomes used to leaving the net when required, or learns to hold it until you can dispatch the rabbit. Whatever happens, if the rabbits are to be of any saleable value, the dog mustn't crunch them in the nets; the dog must respect the net and whatever it holds.

The dog must be completely comfortable and safe with ferrets in any situation. I am assured that this albino ferret passed through the mouth of the young lurcher unharmed. (Craig McCann)

Peripheral vision is required to ensure that the dog takes up a correct and versatile position whilst the ferrets are working. If possible, it shouldn't stand in front of the holes and this is taught when first starting to go ferreting. In open ground, the dog may be left to decide for itself where to stand and you have to trust the dog's decision; it knows before we do where and when the rabbit or ferret is going to surface. The body language of the dog will emit a signal as to which animal is going to surface first: a submissive stance and it is the ferret; an exertive stance and it will be a rabbit. There is nothing wrong with giving the dog the freedom of the warren; just do not let it become accustomed to sticking its head down a rabbit hole, or standing directly in front of the view of the hole. It should just

The dog works alongside the ferrets, not against them. (Steven Taylor)

stand off, out of direct view of the vacating rabbit. In many locations, it is not possible to sit the dog behind or to the side of a netted hole. Trees, fencing, hedging and watercourses all add obstacles to us and our dogs, making reaching the netted rabbit more difficult and this is why the long net is increasingly being used to prevent rabbits escaping more often than they should.

The bread-and-butter relationship between man, dog and ferret has to be strong, but unfortunately in some cases it is weak. I believe it is essential to have a strong bond with my animals, because when they are out in the fields trust plays a big role, especially with the dogs if they are hidden on the other side of a hedge amongst game birds, for example. It is vital that the dogs are broken to birds as well as all other stock. I know many people like their dogs to take feather as well as fur, but this is not possible for me in my profession. I operate in a large shooting county and therefore rely on the people in charge of shoots and land which is shot to pay my mortgage.

It is, of course, imperative that the dog is broken to the ferrets, as one that isn't is nothing but a liability. It is one thing letting a dog experience ferrets, but it is another trusting it when rabbits and ferrets are flying in and out of holes. A dog must be 101 per cent in any situation with your ferrets. The dog must work alongside the ferret, not against it. Let the dog see the ferrets on a daily basis; the ferret therefore becomes part of the furniture, so when the dog experiences the ferret out in the field it is nothing new. The dog will then be able to concentrate on what the ferret is doing, rather than on what a ferret is. This is normally done whilst the dog is still a puppy.

The physical make-up of your ferreting dog tends to be different from county to county to match the needs of the terrain. In my part of Suffolk, the land requires not a large dog but a small, nippy thirty yarder, around 22–24in (56–61cm) in height, as the rabbits don't run more than 30yd (27m) to safety; acceleration as opposed to out and out speed is what is required. A good coat is essential as the easterly winds are very cold in winter. The ground we hunt is sand and clay, not many flints and rocks, and definitely not many hills. The fields have no stock fencing apart from the farmer's friend, barbed wire, mostly hidden in the many thick hedges and deep ditches, so

Concentrating on the rabbit in the hole as opposed to the ferret out of the hole. (Steven Taylor)

a dog with too hard a desire to go crashing about into the hedges will not last the season and a dog injured is no good to me as I haven't the luxury of a kennel full of substitutes.

Intelligence is also a major factor. When is a dog a brainy dog? Some may believe a dog is lacking in intelligence, but it may be the opposite; it may be the owner who simply either cannot see it or cannot understand the dog's level of intelligence. The dog needs to be focused on the job in hand, not wanting to chase game or play when the ferrets are down.

You may have noticed that I haven't mentioned what type of lurcher I prefer; this is because it is the teamwork of dog and owner and their ability to work together in their own terrain which makes the partnership successful. I have seen both good and bad in all types of dog, whatever their shape and size. It is the dog within the dog that does the job, not how it looks. Nothing pleases me more than to be in the company of a well-trained dog; equally, little distresses me more than seeing an unruly dog denying future hunters the chance to experience hunting the fields.

The slow and thorough training of a dog usually ensures many days out in the fields ferreting, with the dog being an integral part of the team. As with all the other pieces of our equipment, storage room is required and time to do it justice, but a dog cannot just be stored and then wheeled out like your nets for the odd day out. Time, money, blood, sweat and tears must be spent during the years it takes to get a young sapling pup through its training until you have had a few seasons under your belt working to the standards that you have set yourself and your dog. Only then has your dog matured into a ferreting dog. I presently have two bitches working alongside me, Maud and Millie. They are doing me proud, although they are not perfect and, to be honest, there is no such dog.

NETS

To ensure that the hard work of the ferret isn't wasted, the rabbits should be caught in whatever nets the ferreter has laid or set. When you take a closer look at the fundamentals of what makes a good net, you will begin to appreciate that there is far more to its make-up than first imagined. Because of the unpredictable nature our terrain, a wide variety of nets of different sizes, shapes and designs is available. The nets are made from either natural or synthetic materials to designs that have been proven over time. The rise in popularity of people knitting their own nets and the increase in the number of commercial outlets,

You must get the dog used to the many distractions encountered whilst ferreting. (Steven Taylor)

Some quality nets from the skilful hands of a quality knitter, Scotland's Bill Snedden. (Steven Taylor)

plus the opening up of the European Union as a free trading marketplace, has had both a positive and a negative effect on the netting market. The wide spectrum of readily available materials is now greater than ever before, so instead of relying on a few importers to sell you their stock, the World Wide Web has ensured that any twine or netting is available from any part of the world and can be purchased from the sanctuary of your home.

The nets used in ferreting are not as complicated as many would have you believe. There are only three separate types of net: a purse net, which is commonly placed over the individual rabbit holes or used to cover certain rabbit runs; a poke net or a double pegger, which is usually a larger version of a purse net but with two pegs instead of one;

and of course the many varieties of long net. Whichever net you use, check them regularly for breakages and repair them accordingly.

Purse Nets

The purse net is designed to have the netting held at either end by rings or sliders; the length of the net is measured from ring to ring/slider and the actual mesh is measured by the half or full mesh. Half mesh is from side to side and full mesh is from stretched knot to knot – for example, a purse net might be 2¼ half mesh or 4½ full mesh. The draw cord is the cord that is threaded through the outside meshes, tied to the top ring (the ring opposite to the end with the peg attached) and freely passed through the bottom ring and tied onto the peg. The net is held in position

In order to work, even the best-made net in the world must be laid correctly. (Steven Taylor)

on the ground by a single peg. The anchored peg gives the draw cord the force of resistance needed to ensure that the net purses (closes) when a rabbit enters the netting, but does not close too easily when a ferret passes through. The draw cord is then firmly held in position, while the net can still move freely.

Poke Nets

The poke net has been around as long as the purse net, but it was designed to operate on larger or multiple holes, often on open ground. The net is basically a larger version of a purse net but with a peg at either end. The net is made up of the same material and mesh size as a purse net but, is normally 5ft or 6ft (1.5/1.8m) in length. With a peg inserted into the ground at each end, the net has two points of resistance as opposed to one, therefore the net draws in from the centre and evenly purses. On a properly set poke net a rabbit has no chance of escape, even if it kicks and struggles. With a purse net having only one point of resistance it is possible to kick and struggle free, especially if the net is too small, because the net is only pursing from one point. When taken into comparison with the purse net, the poke net is more effective. The rabbit is caught at whatever speed it bolts, whereas

the purse net may slip off and present the rabbit with an unexpected avenue of escape, depending on how it was set.

I know that there are two pegs to push into the ground as opposed to the single peg of the purse net and I doubt these nets will ever replace the popular purse net, but I strongly recommend that every ferreter should carry a good half dozen poke nets in his net bag. I normally set a fair few poke nets on runs, setting them on a well-used rabbit run, pegged in at either side and supported by a branch or thick stem of assorted plants that are available. These nets catch well, but a word of warning. The colour of a net placed over a hole is generally unimportant, as the net colour tends to be disguised against a brighter sky and the rabbit is usually in a hurry to bolt, but if a brightly coloured net is placed on a run and the rabbit isn't under pressure, it will sometimes cause the rabbit to shy away from the net.

Long Nets

A long net is exactly what the name implies; it is a length of netting with a top and bottom line threaded through the top and bottom selvage lines (the selvage line is the edge row of meshes which are usually double standard to add strength and durability), held upright by stakes or poles. It comes in two forms, the old (traditional) and the new (fixed net) systems. There is generally 2yd (1.8m) of netting for every 1yd (0.9m) of top and bottom line; this is called the bag or kill. Both methods of long net systems have their advantages and disadvantages, so it is up to the individual's preference as to what system they prefer. Many years ago I started on the traditional method but, after discovering the fixed net method in the early 1980s, I haven't found the need to return to what I regard as a more specialist method.

The oldest method of long netting is the traditional one, which is probably used more by the older generation and traditionalists who go night-time netting as well as ferreting. Night-time netting is a method of

*The caught rabbit has a knack of chewing the net, especially through the top or bottom line.
(Steven Taylor)*

catching the rabbits on their way back to the warren. The nets are set in complete silence between the feeding rabbits and their home, usually with the wind blowing the netter's scent away from the feeding rabbits. The netter then drives the rabbits back towards their home by alerting them of his presence by means of sudden noise or movement. The netter then inspects the net, dispatching the rabbits caught and removing them from the net, which is then cleaned and picked up, ready for another drop. This is very different to daytime netting, where the long nets are used to prevent the rabbits from escaping after being bolted from their warrens during ferreting – do not compare or confuse the two different practices!

The traditional net is carried around on endpins or crooks in one hand. The endpin is inserted into the ground and, with the other hand, the net is laid flat on the ground as the netter walks in the direction that the net is to be set and catch. Once the net is laid down, the other endpin is inserted into the ground. These endpins are vital to give the top and bottom lines the tension needed to keep the net upright once the stakes have been fitted every 5yd (4.5m) or so, depending on the terrain. It is imperative to keep the top line as taut as possible. The stakes are usually made out of hazel or privet, although synthetic ones can be used (but usually the traditional net is worked with traditional materials). With a couple of half hitches holding the bottom and top line in place, the net should be ready to catch. With the net held upright at around 16–18in (40–45cm), the tension between the poles should enable ample bagging of the belly (a part, line or structure that bulges deeply) of the net to catch the rabbits. The rabbits have to run over the net before being caught up in the bagging/belly.

The problem I see with this sort of system is that, whilst ferreting, you may need to surround an area, or set the net at irregular angles. Accordingly, unless you, or your helper, are proficient in laying a long net this way, you will spend a great deal of time and make

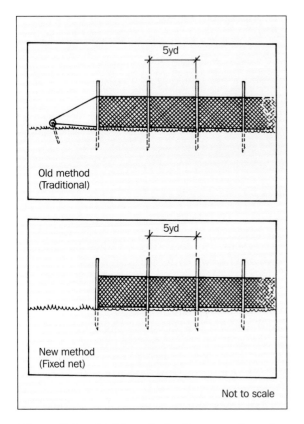

Old method (Traditional)

5yd

New method (Fixed net)

Not to scale

The traditional (old) method relies upon the end pin for the tension to hold the whole net upright, unlike the fixed net method (new), which is self-tensioning.

some noise on or around the warren. As with any net, the setting should be mastered before going out to catch rabbits. If the nets were only small 10yd (9m) nets, placing them through a hedge would be a good way to learn. The advantage of this system is that they are easy to store in a bag, go through or under fences easily, but the main disadvantage is tension. The endpins create the tension in combination with the stakes or poles that keep the net upright. If a rabbit chews through the top or bottom line, or the line hasn't been tied competently, when a rabbit hits the net at speed or a number hit it at the same time, it isn't just that 5yd (4.5m) section that will collapse under the pressure, it could be more. Whatever net you use, it is the tension on the top and bottom lines that is vital for the net to work properly. As I have already stated, it is many years since I have used this method, so if you want to find out more about the traditional method of long-netting I am sure there are many books on the subject written by those with the knowledge to do so.

The newer fixed long net method is just that, the net is fixed permanently to the poles or stakes. Since the early 1970s, when the Scottish rabbit catcher Glenn Waters first brought to the wider world his method of netting, the fixed long net method has been re-invented many times commercially. Initially, the nets were just fixed onto the poles, then carried and dragged, but unless used on clean open ground, debris accumulated in them and meant that the net had to be cleaned after every drop. In the 1980s, Brian Brinded brought us the basket system, using thinner synthetic poles and held together with castration rings. The Quickset Longnetting System brought the old art of long netting into a new era. The nets could be laid quickly and lifted cleanly. The baskets, poles and netting have changed since the original, but the principle of usage hasn't. Today we have the Magnum Trap Company, Bridport Nets and Masterhunter, all selling

OPPOSITE: *The invention of the fixed net method has brought long netting to the masses. (Steven Taylor)*

their own slightly different versions of the fixed net systems. I prefer to use my own customized basket, a collaboration of all the good points of the various types of net and baskets on offer.

I personally prefer the fixed net method, as the vast majority of my netting is daytime but some of the commercial systems that I have used leave a lot to be desired. I usually have either two 50yd (46m) nets or an assortment of 10yd (9m), 15yd (14m) and 25yd (23m) nets. Versatile is what we need to be when ferreting. What is the point of only having 100yd (91m) in one go if you need 10yd or 20yd (18m) at a time? The net would be wasted, so think carefully before buying a huge length of net. These nets can be laid quickly and although speed isn't everything, I like to get the nets down as quickly as I can with the minimum of noise and disturbance to the warrens. The top line is usually around 18in (46cm) high, but this can be altered to suit the terrain by using the grommets on the poles. It is the belly (a part, line or structure that bulges deeply)

of the net that catches the rabbit as well as the bagging. By adjusting the grommets, you can vary the length of shank driven into the ground – a shorter length for hard ground, or a longer length for soft ground. In this way, the pole is far more versatile than a normal net fixed permanently onto a pole with a rubber band, which are hard to move once fitted. If working on smooth ground, ensure that the bottom lines fit to the contours of the ground, as the rabbit will be running lower than when on rough ground.

If the rabbit bites through the top or bottom line, with this method you will only lose the tension and the upright net on that particular section, rather than potentially losing more sections as can be experienced with the traditional method if the net is not laid or set correctly. On the fixed net method, each individual section has its own tension, due to the top and bottom lines being fixed to individual poles rather than being part-reliant upon an endpin and the ability to tie the top and bottom line onto the poles competently every time, as in the old method.

With both methods of long net, the knots securing the line to the poles need to be tied correctly to ensure the net works to its full potential. I have experienced fixed-net methods that have had poor knots tied and these have fallen apart after minimal usage in the field.

The invention of the fixed net method has made daytime netting almost idiot-proof. It takes only a few minutes to become accustomed to setting and picking up this type of system. The net is laid by planning where you want to lay the net, ensuring no obstacles are in the way. Push the first pole into the ground. Walk five paces and the next pole will be ready to place in the ground. This is repeated until you have laid the desired distance; the unused netting remains inside the basket, which is placed on the ground. It is usually better to use a combination of smaller nets to make up the finished distance, as opposed to one large net. By using various sizes of nets in each basket, such as 4 × 25yd (23m); 2 × 25yd and 1 × 50yd (46m); 2 × 50yd; or 6 × 10yd (9m) plus 1 × 25yd, you can position several different nets in various positions or join

them up, as they are not all fixed together in one large length as a 100yd (91m) net would be. A basket can usually carry about 150yd (137m) of set net comfortably, which includes 300yd (274m) of netting. This system provides the versatility to be able to set the net in almost any terrain and at any angle. The vast majority of users of these sorts of system do not go out at night; these nets are used purely for ferreting. In today's marketplace, we are seeing a rise in different names for these nets – one-handed, two-handed, quick-set, speed set, the smaller lengths as hedge or gate nets, ditch nets – but they are all versions of the same thing. One important factor we must not ignore is that not all ferreters or ferreters' helpers are au fait with the use of long nets, so with the fixed-net method being simpler to pick up quickly, a lot of ferreters have increased the quality of their ferreting and the quantity of rabbits caught that could have otherwise escaped. At the end of the day you could have the best net in the world, but if you don't set it in the right place it may as well be the poorest.

Sometimes it is impossible to keep a net clean. (Steven Taylor)

The Trammel Net
The trammel is a variation of a long net, based on the fishing net of the same name. A net of smaller meshes (4in [10cm] full mesh) is set with a wall of larger meshes, usually 9in (23cm) square behind it. The idea of the trammel is to ensure that when the rabbit runs into the net, the smaller meshed net pushes through one of the larger outside meshes and the rabbit is held in a similar fashion to that of a purse-netted rabbit. This type of net is used widely and comes in either a diamond or square outer mesh and a one-wall or double-walled system.

Having only used my trammel net as a small hedge net, I cannot comment on running one hundreds of yards out, but in principle I can see why many use this net, as when a rabbit is caught it definitely isn't going to get out again. However, I cannot see any significant advantages over a well-made and run-out long net. I have used both a single- and a double-walled trammel; the double-walled trammel offers the rabbit an obstacle in the shape of a wall of large meshes before it hits the inner net in order to push through the back net, whereas a single-walled trammel is set with the rabbit running unobstructed and directly into the smaller meshed net and then through the larger meshed net.

Manufacture of Nets
In the past, local net makers simply utilized the readily available local twines, but were handicapped by the availability and quantity of good-quality stock. For the last few decades, the vast majority of ferreters' nets have been made out of nylon (4z or 6z) and later the heavier duty 10z and 12z, or natural material hemp. Spun nylon and spun poly became widely available, but the quality did not fulfil the expectations of its users. In recent years, spun poly and spun nylon have been manufactured to a greater quality and consistency, so it has been widely used for knitting nets.

OPPOSITE: Laying the multi-walled trammel net. (Steven Taylor)

When speaking to the many net makers I know, they are all united in their belief that if a material knits well, it will catch well.

Convenience and cost dictate what is readily available today, with the majority of nets being made from imported sheet netting. I believe that ferreters today tend to fall into the trap of choosing a net based on cost over quality. Commercialism is slowly creeping into ferreting and nets made for the most profit out of the least amount of work are becoming more and more evident. Just because this rubbish is on sale at game fairs, through magazines and on the Internet, it doesn't mean it will be any good, because quite evidently these nets are not. A well-made net from the skilled hand of a proficient knitter is a joy to work; quality will always outlast quantity when used regularly in the field. Finance obviously has a bearing on what type of net is used, but for newcomers one of the most frustrating parts of ferreting will be the laying, picking up debris, losing rabbits and resetting of inferior quality nets, or nets that are clearly not suitable, such as the lightweight 4z nets that I am sure the vast majority of ferreters have used at one time or another.

To make a long net by hand takes many hours, consisting at it does of thousands of knots; it is truly a labour of love. The purse net takes roughly thirty-five minutes for the average netter to make. The problem with hand-made nets is that they are only as good as the person making them, so a nice new net will prove useless if the knots slip, letting the rabbits slip away to safety. For those interested in making their own purse or long nets, individuals and companies such as Bridport Nets (www.bridportnets.co.uk, tel:01308 420927) sell an array of twines, gauges, needles and net-making kits, as well as being experienced knitters themselves.

The problem with much machine-made netting is that it is designed for the fishing industry, that is, to catch fish rather than rabbits. The manufacturers cannot understand why it is so vitally important that the net material doesn't stretch too much. Some machine-made nets stretch more than others and this inconsistency is making more and more people move on to handmade purse and long nets that have been made by proficient people who use different-sized meshes to counteract any stretch that may occur in whatever twine they use. To achieve the best net for the worst situations, the understanding of the strengths and weaknesses of the twines is vitally important. The problem encountered with imported machine-made netting is the lack of quality control. Large batches may be too flexible due to the different batches of nylon used. When these are cut up and sewn onto rings for cheap purse nets, it is harder to notice this flaw than if you make up a long net from such a batch.

The understanding of the net's make-up is as important as the net itself. There is more to a purse net and a long net than just a line and mesh held together. In order to get a versatile net, the quality of the twine used to make it is often overlooked in order to save a few pence. It is a false economy always to buy cheap nets that last for only a few years and lose many rabbits in the process.

Most ferreters (and I was no different) start out using the cheaper, widely available nylon nets, which are made in the more lightweight 4z or 6z. However, the majority of them rarely continue using these beyond the first few times. Progressing onto different twines, the ferreter usually makes his own mind up and settles for the type of net that he is happiest with. Many ferreters prefer to use nets with a mesh size of 2in (50mm) to 2¼in (57mm) half mesh or 4½in (114mm) full mesh, but made in a type of twine that doesn't stretch too much. Before deciding on the mesh size, the materials such as hemp or low-stretch multi-filament twine are getting harder to purchase. A net made of the latter material is sound enough up to a 4½in mesh; polyester is also good because of its low-stretch make-up. The nylons and the many types of spun nylons that are presently popular are a bit more prone to expansion, so it is advisable to drop down to 2in half mesh to compensate for any stretch.

Netting Materials

Netting materials can be separated into four main categories, although other types are used to good effect. All nets will pick up a degree of debris if worked in certain situations, although the lighter nylon nets are a no-go for many ferreters.

Hemp

Being the original material used for nets, hemp is regarded by many with an element of

The poorest nets are often the result of the manufacturer placing profit above proficiency. (Steven Taylor)

nostalgia, but its disadvantages must be considered along with its advantages. Because hemp is a natural material, once it has been harvested and modified into the finished product, great care must be taken to preserve its condition, strength and life. It comes in different thicknesses and by using a wood preservative before it has been knitted, the longevity of the net's life will be increased, although the fact remains that any natural material is open to the abuse of the elements. For this reason, those using hemp nets must ensure that they spend time on the nets' aftercare, which can be laborious as the nets must be dried in natural conditions or fermentation of the strands will occur, which will weaken them. But if treated properly, the material has a lot of life and lays well, so will provide many years of service to you and your team. Hemp nets are often the most expensive but, with proper care, the rabbits caught will pay for the net time and time again.

Nylon

Nylon was originally designed as a synthetic substitute for silk. Nowadays, this material is certainly the most commonly used in ferreting because of the scale and amount of sheet netting that is now being imported for the ferreting and long-netting market. It comes in four main sizes: 4z, 6z, 10z and 12z. The 4z is the smallest and weakest with a breaking strain of 40lb, while the 12z is the largest and heaviest with a breaking strain of 120lb. Although the strongest of the artificial materials and cheaper to manufacture, it is also very elastic. It has the potential to expand anything between 5 and 40 per cent of its original size when put under great stress by the bolting rabbit, hitting it at speed, then returning to its original size when the load has been removed or the rabbit has moved on. This makes it excellent for the fishing industry, but for the ferreting market where stretching nets can mean escaped rabbits, many ferreters drop the mesh size down on their long nets to 2in (50mm) half mesh (4in [100mm] full) to compensate any potential elasticity.

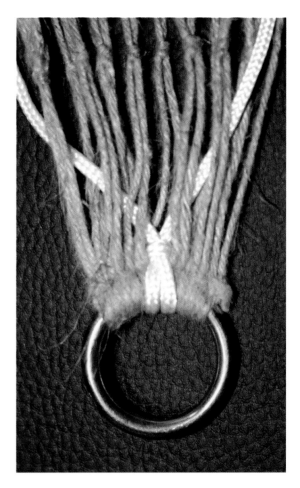

Hemp is often seen as the holy grail of netting materials. (Steven Taylor)

Although no recorded tests have been made on nylon nets, I and many others have seen the rabbits going through the strained net. Some modern nylon is now pre-stretched during its manufacturing process, limiting some but not all of its potential to stretch when put under great stress. Nylon (polamide) has been tested for such elasticity, so information is available about its general elasticity.

Spun Nylon

Spun nylon is another synthetic twine used for its strength. It is a very popular twine for nets, although it does have a tendency to stretch, curl or twist a little. When a material twists or curls, the ease of opening up a purse net can be made more troublesome than it should be. A net should be easy to open, and therefore quicker to lay.

Spun Polyester

Although it has only been around for a relatively short period of time, this man-made synthetic material is becoming very popular amongst ferreters. It is smoother than a natural material, thus is easier to handle, and because of its tighter weave doesn't hold as much water so remains lighter. Ferreters are using this material more and more because it doesn't stretch as much as spun nylon, as during the manufacturing process pre-stretching removes most of the latent elasticity and shrinking is negligible. The biggest advantage over spun nylon and hemp is that it wears better in the harsh environment ferreting offers. Spun polyester threads provide

superior strength and are resistant to sunlight and abrasion when compared to cotton threads of equal size.

Cords and Pegs

The cord, which is normally made out of braided nylon, should be of the right weight for the net and not too light. The cord should fit the contours of the land and so be light or heavy enough to fit your criteria. I have seen some leaded lines recently and I am beginning to wonder where it will all finish. These may weigh down a flimsy net, but the answer is not to use a cheap, flimsy net in the first place. The length of the draw cord is also important, as it not only connects the net to the peg but if the cord is too short, the net cannot be set properly. If the cord is slightly longer all you have to do is wrap the cord around the peg. However, it should not be too long. The role of

The peg must hold firm in order for the net to close properly. (Greg Knight)

this cord is to ensure that once the rabbit has entered the net, the net begins to purse. If the cord is too long the net has to travel before it starts to purse, thus giving the rabbit an avenue of escape. Generally, when the net is about to be set, the distance between the end rings or slider and the peg should be around 6in (152mm), which is enough to be versatile as finding a suitable area to push in the peg is often not as easy as first appears. The draw cord is used to find the outside edge of the net so that it can be opened up easily and quickly and for that reason I like to have a bright colour cord for ease of opening, as the quicker you can open a net, the quicker you can set it and move on.

The peg must suit the ground in which it is to be submerged; many nets are spoilt by the wrong or inappropriate peg being used. The most versatile is the hardwood peg. Pegs are usually wider than the end ring to avoid any possibility of the peg going through the ring, although many nets have larger, heavier end rings to hold the net in position better. The pegs are usually painted in an alien colour so that they are easily visible in all soil and weather conditions. The thinner tent peg (metal spike) is sometimes used, but the only benefit I can see over the wooden peg is for use in rock-hard or frost-covered ground.

The Colour, Shape and Size of Nets

A lot of old-time ferreters used to ferret with nets that were only ten and twelve meshes wide. These nets, which were the same width all the way down from ring to ring or ring to slider, caught great amounts of rabbits. It is a common practice to shape the purse net nowadays, but it is mainly a matter of cost reduction. Saving time and twine will reduce the overheads of each net made, but in an ideal world the net would be made to the satisfaction of the ferreter, rather than the manufacturer.

To many ferreters, a net is simply a net, but those who rely heavily on the net or knit them regard netting completely differently. A net that is nice to knit is usually nice to work with. The craftsmanship that goes into many handmade nets has to be admired – the uniformity of the meshes, the strength of the knots and the end row of meshes that has been sewn onto the rings and how the draw cord has been fitted. The net is usually finished off with a hardwood peg, all smooth and strong, ready for the rigours of a lifetime of ferreting.

Shaped nets work the same as rectangular nets; essentially the net must have been shaped and be the right size for the holes it is used to cover. Rectangular nets are made up from a rectangle of netting, so many meshes wide, and so many meshes deep. The shaped nets are designed on a diamond formation; the top and the bottom rows of meshes are fewer than the broader middle section of the net, gradually fading in and out of formation to make the finished shape. Some people scrimp a bit in the shaping and so have nets that are on the tight side, with the result that if the rabbit doesn't bolt in the middle, the net will not be as versatile or efficient as one that fits properly. Not only must the net be set correctly, but it also must have sufficient bagging to ensure a nice clean action. I have been using a ring on the bottom and a slider on the top for ease of pursing, but how the slider is set depends on how much friction is caused. The wind, ferrets passing through and the balance must all be taken into consideration. If the mesh is too small, the ferret will struggle to move through, making a disturbance, but if the mesh is too large you run the risk of rabbits going through. For this reason, a lot of ferreters do not like their ferrets to work the surface as they tend to disturb the nets too much and resetting each net isn't always a viable option.

The size of the net is also important. Purse nets are usually 3ft (91cm), 3½ft (107cm), or 4ft (122cm) in length whereas the poke nets are usually 5ft (152cm) or 6ft (183cm) in length from ring to ring. The mesh size depends on what size of rabbits you want to catch. 1¼in (32mm) or 1½in (38mm) mesh for young rabbits or 2in (50mm), 2¹⁄₁₆in (52mm),

The bolt trap, in the right place at the right time, has a use. (Nigel Housden / Pinsharp Photography)

2$\frac{1}{8}$in (54mm) or 2$\frac{1}{4}$in (57mm) for adults. As the breeding season alters, so can the choice of the nets used.

The colour of the net is vital, not for the colour-deficient rabbit but for the often short-sighted ferreter. The thinking behind using light- or alien-coloured nets is the ease which they can be spotted when it's time to pick up the nets and move on. The ferreter can easily spot these nets and ensure none are left behind; dull or weathered nets have a tendency to blend into their surroundings. Alternatively, drab nets can be made more visible by using them in conjunction with a brightly coloured draw cord or brightly painted wooden pegs.

So, in short, what makes a good net is one that is easy to handle and opens without spinning. It must be rot-proof and weatherproof (or you must be prepared for the aftercare involved in using hemp). The net should be of a nice weight and have a bit of life about it. Too light a net and it tends to snag on everything and blow about in the wind. However, a net that is too heavy doesn't wrap up well, takes up a lot of room in your bag and if the twine is too thick, it may turn back a cautious rab-

OPPOSITE: Bright nets are not as easily overlooked at the end of the day. (Steven Taylor)

bit due to the fact it can see an obstruction against the skyline. Remember: the best nets are the ones that last forever, hold every rabbit that hits them and don't get lost or end up in the pockets of somebody else's jacket or net bag, but to be honest all the net makers I know have yet to find this magic formula!

CAGE BOLT TRAPS

Cage traps can be and are used to great effect, but only in certain situations. They are placed into the rabbit's entrance/exit hole securely. What the round cage trap brings that a net doesn't is twofold. Firstly, the cage can hold more than one rabbit at a time; secondly, it also holds a ferret, thus stopping the ferret from escaping the warren unnoticed and wandering off. This is great in situations when you are ferreting on roadsides, thick hedges, release pens and other areas where you do not want to lose sight of the surfaced ferret or cannot get to the side of the surfaced ferret in order to provide it with safety from third parties such as cars. A sense of security is given to the ferreter, but there is danger for a ferret walking in on two or three rabbits and this should be avoided. The traps are then removed, stood on their end and, with your

The ferret deserves the best transport available. (Steven Taylor)

arm, stretch down inside and pick the rabbits out one by one, dispatching them as soon as is humanly possible.

FERRET BOXES

The methods of transporting the ferret or ferrets about are clouded by as many opinions and traditional ways as any other aspect of ferreting. There are only two ways of carrying ferrets about in my mind, the right way and the wrong way. The right way is by using a carrying box, the wrong way is in a sack, bag or pocket.

Ferreting has progressed so much that it is rare that a single ferret is worked all day, that is, unless you only have one ferret. The priority is therefore to have a safe mode of transport for the ferrets. The boxes come in different shapes and sizes depending upon how many ferrets are carried. Unlike the older boxes that were extremely bulky, cumbersome and heavy, lightweight boxes are now readily available. The weight of the box is immaterial, because it is the weight of the ferrets within that makes the finished weight. On an average ferreting day, each box I use

houses five jills or a few hobs. I use the bowback boxes, a very old style of carrying box dating back to the turn of the century here in East Anglia. All my boxes have just one single compartment, although many now have two or three separate sections. This is so that it is possible to control the exit of the ferret more easily and to be able to separate ferrets that do not get on. This is fine for travelling, but if you work ferrets that do not get on in a box, they will definitely not get on in the warren and that is counterproductive.

The bowback box has a slightly curved back to fit into the rounded side or back of the person carrying it. The square box, which has a flat back, doesn't fit into a curve so therefore has more movement. The ferrets must be able to feel safe during transit and not be tossed and spun about just before you expect them to work their little backsides off for you. When in transit, the ferrets can relax or sleep. Ferrets transported in such a way outperform stressed ferrets in inadequate transport every time. Obviously, the more ferrets you use, the

OPPOSITE: The best seat and view in the house. (Steven Taylor)

more or larger boxes you will need, but the more you carry, of course, the heavier the load will be.

Cages, bags and even drainage piping have been tried but if they were as successful as the carrying box, all the sporting magazines would be full of adverts for such equipment. To ensure that you have a good box, you should follow these guidelines. Make sure it is made out of good, well-tested materials such as external or marine plywood. The box needs to have a fail-safe lock fitted to the lid to avoid the ferrets escaping after a good scratch at the lid. Ensure that no noticeable gap is apparent between the lid and the back of the box, as rain will soak the ferrets if there is a gap of any size. Good ventilation is important in the warmer weather, though there should not be too many holes and not in an area where the ferrets can get chilled. I always have the holes on the side of the top half; this ensures that the front and backs are solid and the wind and rain cannot get into the ferrets. A good strap finishes off the box and with a good lick of animal-friendly wood preservative, the ferret box is in my opinion unbeatable.

Inside the car the ferrets are carried around in a big cage, cat carriers or a large, airy wooden chest box and transferred to individual boxes depending on how many are needed upon arrival. All the car transport boxes have a water bottle fitted. The number of ferrets carried varies from a couple to two dozen or more when myself and a few friends tackle the bigger warrens.

The best use of the ferret box has nothing to do with ferrets. It is used to sit on and have a cup of tea whilst ferreting. That is why whatever it is made from, ensure that it is up to your weight!

OTHER ITEMS

Knives
No ferreter should ever leave the house without a good, sharp knife – a versatile item used to gut or leg the rabbit so you can hang them

or carry them about comfortably. To leg a rabbit, a small incision is made in between the lower tendons of one of the rear legs, and the other leg placed through; the tendon is usually then slit on the leg that has just gone through to ensure it doesn't slip off. The knife can also be used to cut through any impeding obstacle such as baling twine, or to cut the sharp thorns of a stick for you to locate a rabbit with if it is just out of arm's reach after it has been dug to.

Spades
The spade is probably as important to a day's ferreting as the ferrets themselves. If you forget the spade, how are you going to recover your ferrets from the earth if a dig is required? As with most of your equipment, the spade must be suited to your terrain and be robust enough to withstand whatever the day's ferreting challenges it with.

You would be amazed at just how many different soils you will encounter, from sand right through clay to heavy rock, chalk or, worse, roots. Your spade must be practical, strong and have a head designed for digging, that is, sharp, clean and sturdy. The spade must be designed to dig efficiently into whatever surface you find yourself ferreting. Many different designs of spade are available, but the size of the head is as vital as the length of the shaft. A long-handled spade will prove to be impractical in a lot of areas. The normal spade size is around 3ft (91cm) in length from handle to head. I normally have a few spades handy, from a small spade designed for light work, right through to a metal-shafted, angled-head spade for the heavier sort of dig. I use a metal-shafted tool as I find these to be more hard-wearing than the wooden ones.

Look after your spade and it will look after you. Ensure that you keep the cutting blade sharp and the head oiled in order to keep it clean. I like the head to be shaped slightly, as this cuts into the ground easier than a standard square head. Accompanying the spades in the car is a 2ft (60cm) heavy metal spike. I use this to break into or open up

A variety of digging equipment assembled, just in case. (Ivan Ambrose)

extremely hard surfaces. Digging in the winter can be hard, plus wet surfaces often hide a dry and hard subsurface, especially around trees and hedges where the roots soak up all the moisture. Ground driven over by tractors or heavy vehicles can compact the soil the same as frozen earth. These may all require a little persuasion in softening up prior to the spade being deployed.

Probes

The probe is usually a long metal bar with a 'T' handle, although I often use an old fibre-glass long net pole. Its job is to probe the soil to find the exact location of a pipe in the warren. When digging, I find these invaluable, as sometimes the warren's pipes will be running alongside or over the top of each other and it is easy to reach the wrong conclusion when digging. The safety aspect of using one is also invaluable, as the spade of an overenthusiastic digger can be potentially lethal to the unfortunate ferret. However, you should only use a probe with a rounded and blunt end, to ensure that you avoid accidental injury to your ferret.

Bags

Your equipment will have to be carried around in something and a good old-fashioned game bag will take some beating. Cheap, weatherproof and well constructed, these will carry your nets, food and flask, as well as those little odds and ends you may find yourself with. Many different types of bags are used, from falconers' vests to pouches or homemade carrying pouches that sit snugly and only carry nets.

Clearance Tools

As the climate changes and the amount of foliage increases, the need to clear undergrowth has become more necessary. Machetes, bill hooks and slashers now rank among secateurs as vital pieces of clearance equipment.

Digging Bags

I normally carry about inside my large net bag a smaller bag containing my digging tools. I find a torch essential to actually see what is going on down the hole once my head and shoulders have blocked out the light. The presence of light in a dark tunnel also catches the attention of the ferret, making it easier sometimes to recover one before drawing the rabbits out. The bag also contains gloves to protect against sharp objects, a knife, secateurs to trim and cut objects such as twine or roots, a few sticks used to locate a rabbit that has strayed or been pulled back after I have broken through to the pipe, and a flask to provide a nice hot drink.

Mobile Phones

Due to the isolated venues and unpredictable weather that are part and parcel of ferreting, it is always advisable to have handy a mobile phone with good coverage. Nothing is more annoying than having a phone going off when you are aiming for quiet, so put it on silent or even switch it off, but at least you will have a means of communication if an accident occurs to you or any of your animals.

OPPOSITE: The day of the thick coat has come to an end. (Steven Taylor)

Clothing

Because of the unpredictability of the weather, it is often wise to find out in advance what the weather patterns are expected to be, although with regularity these tend to be wrong. The clothes that the ferreter wears will play an enormous part in the day's ferreting. Concentration wanes if you are too cold or too warm, so it pays to know what you are comfortable wearing and whether it will suit the harsh environment in which the ferreting will be conducted. The modern trend to use head to toe camouflage doesn't make you a better ferreter, but wearing bright colours may make you a poorer one. Sticking out like a sore thumb may help you if you are on the peaks, fells or moors as the passers-by will assume you are just another walker, but in the majority of scenarios it is preferable to blend into the surroundings to avoid spooking the rabbits into going back to ground. Usually the clothes that are worn for ferreting are old and tatty, so that you are not fussed when they get torn and extremely dirty. Nowadays, the preference tends to be not for thickness but for layers of fleeces and tops, utilizing modern fabrics, but only if they are suitable firstly for the weather and secondly for the hedges that have to be gone through during the day's ferreting.

The head is the one part of the body we tend to forget about protecting. The greatest loss of body heat is through the head, so if we take care of the head, the rest of our body will not feel as cold. Woolly caps or hats, bushman-style rimmed hats or a weatherproof baseball cap all fit the bill. If, like me, you wear glasses, you will need a brim on your hat to protect the glasses from the rain. It helps if you can see what you are doing.

The next most important part of your anatomy to protect is your feet. Keeping these warm and comfortable is essential; you won't have the luxury of stomping about to keep warm, as this would definitely send the rabbits into alert mode. I prefer to wear a good pair of walking boots where I can, as I find that I can dig better due to the substantial but

lightweight soles they now have. Wellington boots very seldom have a hard enough sole for digging regularly, so when purchasing any footwear with a view to ferreting, check the soles, their waterproof capability and whether they are truly comfortable enough to stand around in for long periods of time.

Once your head and feet are sorted out, you will need to look at what protects the rest of your body. As I stated earlier, with a different and changeable climate we must be prepared for really cold, wet or windy weather and possibly all in the same day. Unless it has been or is raining, I generally use some old ex-army Gore-tex overtrousers as they are light, waterproof and relatively cheap to buy, so if I go through a pair or two in a winter, it is no real hardship. Wax overtrousers are good if you are in and out of thick, prickly hedges or bushes, but if you are standing around all day, they can be cold and heavy. A lot of people just use chaps of whatever material and these can be good, although as chaps are designed just for the legs, when you sit down on the wet ground for a cuppa, you will discover why they were designed for walking and riding and not for sitting down in.

The jacket or jackets that are used must be the same as the trousers – quiet to move in, weatherproof and comfortable to be in all day. It is no good if you are constantly worrying about being cold or wet when you should be concentrating on the ferrets. With the development of modern fibres and materials, we are no longer reliant upon wax jackets to keep us dry, although, to be honest, they still are one of the better jackets to wear for all-round protection. When looking at your ferreting jacket, think about the bushes, hedges and trees that will try their hardest to part this clothing from your back. The jacket was designed to protect us and not be left behind in tatters inside a hedge line. A lot of the

OPPOSITE: It is imperative that you keep warm and dry. (Nigel Housden/Pinsharp Photography)

modern sporting clothing is fine until it gets physical contact with sharp and prickly objects, then we see just why the ferreter wears old and tatty clothing. It is a good idea to have a few items of spare clothing inside the van or car, just in case any accidents do happen. Gloves are not really suitable as the ferrets' claws get stuck in them, they get wet and your fingers cannot function with the dexterity you require, but at the end of the day the choice is yours.

Food and Drink

We all know how we love a warm drink, especially when the ferret has laid up or you want to tempt fate and get the ferret or rabbit out. By ensuring you have a drink for the dogs and ferrets and not just yourself, you will be prepared for the unpreparable, as you never know what is around the corner. A good lunch box will make sure that you keep your energy levels up and concentration focused, especially if you have had a few digs.

Hygiene and First Aid

Ferreting is practised in a natural environment and while the native animals are used to those conditions, we unfortunately are not. You will be working in an environment that is neither clean nor hygienic, so a little care must be taken before, during and at the end of the day. If you are anything like me, at the end of a day's ferreting your hands will be filthy, cut and scratched, as well as stinging from contact with nettles. It always pays to carry in the car a good first-aid kit and some water, soap and disinfectant to clean the worst off your hands, or in case you have to clean a cut or abrasion in preparation for a dressing to be applied. Our countryside is full surprises that can do you and your animal great harm. Becoming more hygienic doesn't take a lot of time, but it will prevent any nasties building up under the skin that could prevent you from going out ferreting in the future.

CHAPTER FIVE

Ferret Retrieval Devices, Methods and Options

Since domestication brought us the ferret, the ways in which they have been worked have always been portrayed as relatively simple. In a perfect world, the ferret is released into the rabbit warren, all the rabbits bolt and the ferret duly returns to the surface. If life was this simple, we would have no rabbits left, but in reality the rabbit dictates whether or not it's going to bolt freely. If the rabbit feels safe in its home, it will stay put. We then have the problem of retrieving a reluctant ferret. Mankind domesticated a carnivorous predator to work for him and then was foolish enough to release it many feet under the ground in search of its quarry. The problem of how to retrieve the ferret is as old as ferreting itself. When referring to retrieval systems, I refer to a system that should ensure that you retrieve the ferret there and then and not a day or two later.

In the early days of ferreting, many ferrets were simply lost or left to fend for themselves because they showed the tenacity and characteristics of any predator and stayed underground with the rabbit. Many simply wandered off into some undergrowth when out of sight of the people ferreting. Later, ferreters fixed lines to the ferrets via a collar or harness, but this limited the hunting range of the mustelid. Some ferrets were fitted with a muzzle or cope, or had their carnivorous teeth removed so that they couldn't kill underground, but this didn't stop them staying with the rabbit and attempting to turn the bottled-up animal with their powerful claws. The ferret was still in subterranean territory. The ferreter had no idea where the ferrets were or how deep. What was required was a successful way of finding and retrieving them. The alternative for the ferret at this time was to end up trying to fend for itself after being left behind, but only if it was lucky enough to get the muzzle or cope off. If not, the ferret simply starved to death or was attacked and eaten by one of its many predators.

At that time in our history, the landscape was much quieter, the population a lot smaller and the rabbits would have reacted to this and bolted more freely due to the general lack of disturbance. It was possible to ferret in quiet countryside and hear where the action was happening. The warrens were normally 3ft to 4ft (0.9m to 1.2m) deep so sound would travel, giving a good indication of where the ferret was scrabbling at the rabbits.

The majority of working ferrets were, and still are, the jills. These female ferrets are generally smaller, quicker and tend not to stay with a rabbit for any great amount of time if stuck in a stop end, whereas the hobs tended to stay with the bottled-up rabbits and these were the ones that got left behind. Over time and experience, the ferreter decided to use the hob's reluctance to leave or share a rabbit to their advantage, and the hob ferret was used to locate another that was underground with a rabbit.

It was common for the ferret to have its teeth snapped off. (Author)

THE FERRET LINE

No one knows exactly when the ferret line was created. This system wasn't without its flaws, however, as it would only work in the smaller warrens. The line that was used had to be weatherproof, lightweight and not too heavy for the ferret to drag around underground. Beeswax was often applied to a very thin but strong twine in order to preserve and grease the fibres together. A natural untreated twine was too unreliable and prone to breaking. Many cords were simply too heavy to move over and around the roots surrounding the warren's pipes. It has been suggested by the ferreters of old that only a small percentage actually bothered to use a liner (the ferret attached to the line), as it was too much work and a waste of valuable time allocated to going ferreting. Bells were used, tied around the ferrets' neck and with the stillness of the air, the bells could be heard whilst moving. However, they didn't offer any accuracy when it came to digging as a bell often became clogged up with the soil and therefore wouldn't ring.

Blocking holes and leaving boxes open or setting box traps were the method at the time to capture lost or wayward ferrets. In areas heavily set with gin traps, many ferrets succumbed to the metal jaws that were set for rabbits, because sometimes they had been set within the burrow. They were set at about arm's length and fastened to a piece of wood for easy removal. I know of a few young fer-reters of that time who caught their fingers on traps set for rabbits. We will never know the truth, but I suspect a lot of ferrets died after meeting these indiscriminate traps above or below the warrens.

How a Liner was Used

Once it was decided that a ferret needed re-trieving, the liner was called upon. This male ferret was raised and acclimatized for such a job. He was a loner who viewed whatever he came across in a jealous manner, refusing to share what he hunted. For many years this was the most successful method of retrieving a recalcitrant ferret from an underground warren, although it was laborious and time-consuming as a lot of separate holes had to be dug. Continually stopping ferreting for long periods of time to retrieve a lost ferret handi-capped the day's ferreting, which is why only a few practised the use of a liner on a regular basis.

Attached to the ferret was a collar or har-ness, usually made of leather and with a swivel attached to hold the chosen twine or cord. In later years, this cord was knotted at intervals of 3ft (0.9m), but initially a piece of coloured cotton was sewn through the cord, so that the ferreter feeding the line out could count the amount of strands used, thus cal-culating the length of cord used. The cotton wouldn't get caught on a tight root like a knot, so was deemed safer. Once released into the depths of the earth, the ferreter counted the amount of knots or cotton flecks/lines that disappeared with the ferret. When the line ceased to move, it was generally an indica-tion that the hob had found what it had been looking for. A scuffle usually occurred, with the hob pushing off the other ferret from the rabbit. Usually, the missing ferret resur-faced, but the liner would still be with his ill-gotten gain. The hard work was now just beginning as a length of stick was pushed at arm's length down the burrow and a marker placed into the ground directly above the end of the stick. A hole was then dug down to the

line; this was repeated until the ferreter came across the liner, hopefully with a rabbit. This method obviously had many drawbacks, some of them potentially lethal to the ferret.

When I first began ferreting with old farmer Bob and we used a liner, we only worked war-rens with a few holes and usually only smallish warrens that weren't too deep. Those that I personally know who ferreted large warrens several decades ago rarely used a liner, as it wasn't practical, so they used a different re-trieval device, a trap box (see below). One other drawback of the liner system was that when the ferret was released and 25yd (23m) of line was taken underground it didn't mean that the ferret was necessarily 25yd away. That depended upon the depth of the warren and in which direction the pipes took the fer-ret. For decades, this was the only method of ferret retrieval, but, as technology improved, so did the way we worked our ferrets.

THE INVENTION OF THE ELECTRONIC FERRET RETRIEVAL DEVICE

One of the biggest changes in ferreting culture has been the invention of the electronic ferret-finder system. The most important function of any system is to give the ferreter the ability to recover the ferret when required and be-cause of the nature of how the ferret works, the rabbit or rabbits should also be retrieved at the same time. The unfortunate by-prod-uct of this system is the way in which many ferreters perceive it should be used. This isn't the fault of the system, but of the people who use it in a certain manner. In my experience and opinion, the advantages of this electronic system far outweigh any disadvantages cited in the argument against employing it. The ferreter's continuous inability to read the fer-ret finder's instructions properly is giving an accurate account of the equipment's capabil-ity. In order to give sensible guidance and advice based upon actual working experienc-es of the equipment, the equipment must be used correctly in the first place. Incorrect use and guidance has undoubtedly taken away a certain amount of field craft from ferreting. With proper usage, these systems are as valuable as the ferret and spade and in my opinion or company, no ferret should or would be put to ground without one fitted.

With the growth in modern technology has come the invention of many electronic devices to influence how, where and when we carry out certain actions. As humans, we use sport as a means of relaxation, with golf being one of the most popular. It is through golf that we were inadvertently given the initial introduction to the piece of equipment that has revolutionized ferreting. In the late 1960s, a device was invented to assist golfers to find their golf balls when hit into the rough. In the game of golf, a lost ball brings a penalty to the score, but also a financial loss with a replacement ball being necessary. Stephen Alexander Horchler designed and then patented his invention to assist finding lost golf balls in 1971 and this was soon to be seen on national television, featured on a programme called *Tomorrow's World*.

Watching with great interest, as were many others, as the technology for the future was being put through its paces, was a gamekeeper in Norfolk called John Lawrence. Mr Lawrence had one of those eureka moments that very few of us have and even fewer act upon. If he had decided to make a cup of tea, walk the dog or clean out his ferrets at that moment during its airing, it might have been years before we were given an electronic system for finding ferrets.

The golf ball finder was called 'the Bleeper'. It consisted of a transmitter unit fitted inside the elastic filling of a golf ball and a hand-held receiver unit. When the ball was lost, the receiver unit, similar to a transistor radio in size, shape and function, tracked the transmitted signal and located the ball. This piece of electronic equipment was designed to be used by the golfer when he was within 8ft (2.4m) or so of the lost golf ball. It was a revolutionary device, but what Mr Horchler had failed to take into account was the spirit in which golf is played. Such a device wasn't welcomed by the authorities or the golfing

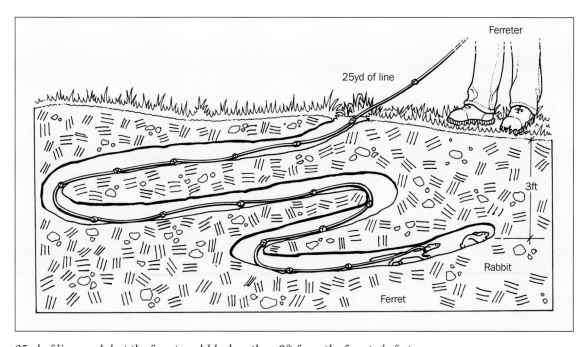

25yd of line used, but the ferret could be less than 3ft from the ferreter's feet.

West country ferreter Bob Lee's original bleeper box. (Bob Lee)

OPPOSITE: *X marks the spot. (Steven Taylor)*

community at that time; it was considered that if a ball was lost, it remained lost and no electronic device could or should be used to find it. Unless every single ball was fitted with this device, a golfer using them would have an unfair advantage over those who didn't have them.

For that reason, the golfing Bleeper failed to take off, but Mr Lawrence saw the benefits of such a system and how he could adapt this device to find his ferrets when they stayed underground. He contacted Euronics, the company making the Bleeper, and, after a meeting, had a few samples sent for him to examine. Mr Lawrence's young sons had the job of opening up these golf balls so that their father could see what the internal workings were like and if they could be adapted to suit a ferret. The internal electronic workings were then attached to a leather collar for the ferret to wear. The transmitter unit was left untouched.

Because of its failure as a golf product, after high expectations and the quantity of stock produced, Euronics was glad to offload what was, to them, a useless item. John Lawrence saw them as anything but useless and got

to work in adapting them for ferreting. The amount of stock purchased would see out the Bleeper's history, with it ceasing production in the early 1980s. Many have thought that the name Bleeper was given to this device when used for ferreting, but it was in fact the original name for the golf ball finder. Mr Lawrence didn't invent this device or name it; he simply adapted it to his requirements.

The newly adapted equipment wasn't without its problems, though. The first version had a fixed battery inside the resin protecting the workings and this had a very limited and unreliable lifespan. The second version replaced the sealed battery unit with a battery unit with a rechargeable capability, but this was again unreliable. In 1975 John Lawrence moved from Norfolk, taking a part-time job in Kent so that he could give more of his time to the ongoing development of the Bleeper system and to sell other ferreting equipment to the ferreting fraternity. The third version of this collar had a television coax connector fitted to a hearing-aid style battery. It was now possible to replace the battery, giving the collar a much longer lifespan in the field. By the early parts of 1976 the final version of the

Bleeper's collar was in circulation and many other sections of industry were interested in using such a device in other capacities. Major drain blockage companies, communication and cable laying companies were keen to find some device that would hurry up the process of finding faults underground and save the costly digging of unwanted excavations.

The Bleeper finally succumbed not only to the financial pressures of the early 1980s marketplace, but also to the continuing problem of unreliability. For a few years after the Bleeper's demise, other devices were on the market, not all of them of better quality or more reliable. Some of these other early ferret finders or locators were very crude and some used a transistor radio as a receiver. The ferreter using the latter could also enjoy listening to the radio or local constabulary whilst trying to find his ferrets. This may sound amusing to some today, but back

then it was infuriating. This system was renowned for its unreliability, but at least it gave the ferreter an idea of where the ferret was. Whether or not he could then successfully find and dig up the ferret was down to individual skill. But, as in all walks of life, the increase in the technological world has given us better and more reliable equipment designed by people skilled in the electronics field, and so these early variable devices have been consigned to the history books along with the original idea of the Bleeper for the recovery of golf balls.

During the mid 1970s in the county of Suffolk, a telephone engineer called Paul Walker was working on a similar idea to help out a friend. He had a constant problem in reliably finding his ferrets and unfortunately some were being lost. A chance conversation over a pint in his local hostelry in Woodbridge prompted Paul to find a solution.

(From left to right) One of the first ferret finders to be built, which evolved into the more commonly seen centre version, then to one of the last Mk1s made by Deben. (Steven Taylor)

THE PAUL WALKER/DEBEN ELECTRONIC FERRET FINDER: THE MK1

Since the early days of building the first ferret finders in his bedroom, Paul Walker has gone on to create a successful business selling ferret-finder sets and other equipment. The Deben Electronic Ferret Finder in one form or another has been around since 1978. In the years since the Mk1 was first manufactured, its inner circuitry has had eight different electronic versions. The original components have all been changed and superseded. In the harsh reality of industry, no material or component will be manufactured if it isn't a viable economic practice. As the world outgrew the simple electronic components utilized to make the original ferret finders, they have been replaced without the unsuspecting ferreters noticing the difference. Deben has ensured that the finished product wasn't affected by the enforced changes in technology, but these changes signalled the end of the manufacture of the Mk1 Ferret Finder in 2005, although they can still be repaired if the spare parts are available. The ferret finder had to move with the times; the nation's ferreters had the ability to surf the net, possess mobile technology at their fingertips, but were, until this point, still reliant upon technology dating back to the 1970s to find their ferrets. Over the years, many ferreters offered constructive improvements to the Mk1 set; the resulting changes were made and in late 2004, the updated version was the Mk2, which was superseded in 2005 by the Mk3. Deben's website is www.deben.com, and its telephone number Tel: 0870 4422600.

The original Mk1 ferret finder was a good set in its heyday, but over time its limitations were exposed. When we look at the sets and compare them in the cold light of day, it is evident why thirty-year-old technology has been bettered and replaced with a more modern, maintenance-free and reliable unit. Even sentimentality isn't going to hide the painful fact that it is a dated and flawed unit

when compared with the modern-day version. Technology has moved on at an accelerated pace and if we want to progress and continue to achieve our goals, most times it is necessary to move with it. I have heard all the arguments regarding why the Mk1 remains better than the Mk3. Many ferreters use the Mk1 simply because it is the traditional box they have always used; many use it because they do not like change and others because it does not warrant spending money to replace something that still works for them. I can understand the latter, but I have had contact with many ferreters who have been put off by hearsay or haven't read the operating instructions properly, if at all. The older we become, the less tolerance we tend to have towards any changes in technology. It took me nearly three weeks of daily use to understand fully and be satisfied with how to get the best out of the new Mk3 system. Of course, it is perfectly acceptable to continue with the Mk1 version; the problems will come when they one day need repairing and there are no longer any parts available.

Paul Walker produced the first Mk1 set in 1978. At the time, it was state-of-the-art technology and its usage revolutionized ferreting for the masses. The set comes in two parts, the receiver and the transmitter. The receiver is a hand-held box with a dial on one side. The Mk1 receiver was originally manufactured in a matt battleship grey colour. This box could be, and invariably was, easily lost, so some ferreters painted them a bright colour such as orange to make them more visible. The design of the receiver box is such that it is only partially weatherproof. This is down to the fact that it has a dial (wheel) sticking out of one side, exposing the inner workings of the box to the elements. The wheel is the on/off switch, as well as the depth gauge. Zero is when it is clicked off and then when it is clicked on, a sticker on the wheel marks the calibrated depths. One of the most common problems reported was either customers asking for a new sticker or wanting the wheel repaired.

Many ferreters added a bit of varnish to protect the self-adhesive sticker from the elements and this ensured a longer lifespan for the sticker; others scratched the dial numbers onto the edge of the dial. Although reassuring to the ferreter, this offered no resistance to the problems that the set experienced whilst working in certain environments. A series of blips reminiscent of a Geiger counter informs the user of its depth and how many collars through a speaker fixed internally. Due to the limited technology of the components, the receiver may experience interference from its surroundings. Metallic objects, electric wires used to pen animals and airborne signals from transmitters can be picked up. Not only was this annoying, but would usually occur at a time when the device was needed most. I have experienced on a number of occasions a ferreter wrongly assuming that this interference was the noise the device should make and instead of turning the set off and starting again, they continued with this prolonged crackling noise. Although Mk1 had a tendency to pick up stray interference from time to time, unlike its competitors, this box was reliable when looked after. With regular services to ensure that the set worked to its design of either 8ft (2.4m) or 15ft (4.6m) and with careful handling in the field, I know of original boxes from 1978 that still operate correctly to this day. Powered by a 9V PP3 battery, the way in which this system works ensures a long battery life.

At the time of the original launch, the collar was very up-to-date technology. They continued to work successfully so nothing really required changing for many years. Human error was at fault in many cases when these transmitter collars failed to perform. Many used cheaper or free batteries that fitted the collar but failed to be the right strength required. With the wrong batteries fitted, the signal isn't as reliable or calibrated as it should be. The main culprit was a hearing-aid battery, usually a zinc air model, which was 1.4V as opposed to the proper 1.55V batteries recommended.

It has been found to be a good idea to wrap a little electrical tape around the cap in order to ensure that when the rabbit kicks out at the ferret, it can't loosen the cap and thus stop the signal. The tape protecting the collar has to be wrapped in the opposite direction to the screw cap in order to stop any turning, which would prevent the connection from sending out the signal to the receiver box. This tape also protects the collar's workings from dirt and grime and from upsetting the mechanics of the cap. The whole module is set in resin with a screw cap connector to hold the battery in place and is held onto the ferret's neck by a leather collar. If not correctly cared for or treated with a leather solution, these leather collars crack and break over time. The holes already punched are just as a guide; for a proper fit, a new set of holes might need to be punched.

At the time of writing, these collars and receivers are still being used and repaired by literally thousands of ferreters up and down the country and abroad. The demand for these Mk1 sets is such that on popular Internet auction sites, a collar or receiver can demand as much as, if not more than, the price of a brand new Mk3. To many ferreters, the Mk1 is the holy grail of ferret finders and whatever opinions or persuasions are put over, they will only have eyes for this little grey box. To me, if I can embrace technology to help me catch more rabbits and lose less time in finding my ferrets, I will. Being nostalgic will not put more rabbits in the bag, but consistently being able to find your ferrets underground with a rabbit will. The Mk1 receiver can pick up the Mk3 collars to an uncalibrated depth of 11ft (3.4m), so for die-hard fans of the little grey box, it isn't all bad news.

Mk1 Ferret Finder
Operating Instructions
Although this set is no longer widely available, any sets sold now will probably have no written instructions, although the seller will most probably pass on a few hints or tips on its usage. It is easy for this set to be used

incorrectly or inefficiently if the user hasn't been shown the error of his ways. I have witnessed the Mk1 being used incorrectly on many occasions. The Mk1 set comes in three forms but only two depths, 8ft (2.4m) (standard and micro) and a 15ft (4.6m) model. The two 8ft sets use the same receiver, but the 15ft set requires a 15ft receiver with a calibrated 15ft sticker on the wheel, although the 8ft collar can be used with a 15ft receiver but will be uncalibrated. The difference between them is the size of the collar transmitters, with the micro being the smallest, the 15ft the largest and the standard 8ft sandwiched in-between.

If you have purchased a second-hand set, the first thing you must do is put in new batteries. To replace the battery in the receiver box, simply unscrew the four corners of the reverse side and remove the covering plate. Insert a new 9V PP3 battery and fix the lid on again with the screws tight. To place a new battery in the collars, loosen and remove the collar cap and insert a battery to suit the collar with the negative (–) side facing downwards touching the rivet set inside the resin on the module attached to a leather collar. This must only be tightened 'finger tight'. If the cap is tightened too much, the rivet will puncture the battery and thus not work correctly.

The system works by fitting the transmitter collar to the ferret's neck with the module under the ferret's chin. To locate your ferret, turn the receiver on full and sweep across the ground at a constant height from side to side until a signal is picked up. The device will be bleeping like a Geiger counter at this point. You must then reduce the depth of the signal by turning the wheel's depth gauge downwards, reducing the volume (sensitivity) and following the signal, sweeping from side to side at a regular level, moving across the signal to gain maximum coverage of the ground until you are at the minimum depth at which you can pick up in the one spot. You are now directly above the ferret.

This final step is normally done with the receiver moving around about 1ft (30cm) above

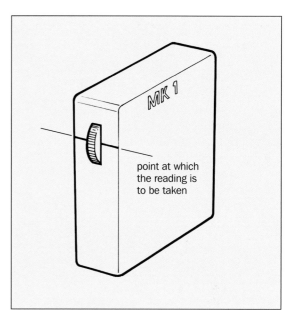

The true reading of the Mk1 is on the marked line in the centre of the dial.

the ground, ensuring that many tall ferreters have bad backs. It is necessary to bend over because of the 8ft range; if you stand up this will take half of the range away. However, this need to stoop can be overcome by taping the receiver onto a pole.

The true reading is in the middle of the wheel (see diagram), but many ferreters use the bottom of the dial or the top as a guide. Whatever part of the wheel you use, as with any ferret-finder set, it is only an estimate and will vary with different soil conditions and battery strength.

THE MK2 FERRET FINDER

In September 2004, Deben released a new set, the Mk2 Ferret Finder. It was the result of technological advances combined with the ideas and constructive criticism aimed at the Mk1 given by many ferreters who required a better system. At the outset, Deben was looking for a set that carried all the ingredients needed to last the harsh environment that ferreting offers such equipment. The changes included a brightly coloured hand-

The Mk2 and collar. (Steven Taylor)

set, increased signal strength and a slimline collar. An increased range ensures that the ferreter no longer has to bend over to use the ferret finder, but can operate it standing upright. Included in the Mk2 was a new addition, an anti-interference circuit to block out any unwanted attentions from electric wires, metallic objects and all those other irritants that rendered the original Mk1 unusable at times. Expectations were high and I had the privilege to take the prototype set and its designers for a trial, a full day's ferreting in Suffolk. Unfortunately, a day's testing in the field cannot and did not show up the faults and weaknesses that a hard season's ferreting would.

The hand-held receiver is contained within a streamline, weatherproof casing with an on/off switch on one side and a search and locate switch on the other which is clearly embossed onto the moulded casing. The search and locate mode was another of the new addi-tions, giving the ferreter a chance to search for and locate his ferrets with the minimum of movement, thus preventing disturbance to the warren at this time. Although you are probably never going to dig 18ft (5.5m) down, at least you know where the ferrets are. To ensure that the receiver is weatherproof, all switches are magnetic reed; this means that there are no moving parts for the weather's elements to find their way into the internal workings (unlike the Mk1) and also to raise the reliability of the set. The depth reading is shown on an LED (light-emitting diode) panel in conjunction with a series of high-pitched blips on the hand-held receiver. One of the major strengths of the new model was the ex-tra distance that was gained for its signal, a jump from 8ft (2.4m) to 20ft (6m).

Unfortunately though, problems did arise and although Deben corrected them, the com-pany soon realized this version wasn't what was required to replace the Mk1 and stopped production to concentrate on an upgraded version called the Mk3. However, there are still many Mk2 sets in use and working for those who enjoy their ferreting.

The main problem was that the increase in range to 20ft (6m), combined with the anti-interference circuit, caused a drain on the batteries. As a result, battery life was not what was to be expected for day-to-day use in the field. I found the collar's battery life to be around twenty hours, but instead of the LEDs slowly fading with the power loss, the system switched off with little or no warning when the battery failed. Another practical problem was that the receiver could only pick up one collar at a time due to the way in which the anti-interference circuit worked, blocking out everything except the signal of a single transmitter collar.

The Mk2 set has a search and locate mode that means you can search for your ferrets within a range of 20ft (6m) and when you are within 10ft (3m) of the signal source, you switch from the search mode to the locate mode. This enables the ferreter to locate his ferret to within 1ft (30cm), though this is another problem as 1ft when digging can be the difference between success and failure, or, more to the point, a ferret being retrieved or not.

Mk2 Ferret Finder Operating Instructions

When using the Mk2, ensure that the transmitter's (collar) battery compartment is clean and dry. The housing of the Mk2 transmitter is black, attached to a collar made from synthetic webbing very similar to a watchstrap. To obtain extra protection for the battery connection, place some insulating tape around the joins on the collar's housing. A 9V PP3 battery powers the receiver. Rechargeable batteries can be used for the receivers, but, as with all batteries, once the power starts to lower, the receiver will produce a less accurate reading.

To remove the battery, take the cover off the rear of the unit and insert a new battery as shown by the diagram on the inside of the

battery housing. Once replaced, the receiver can then be checked to see if it is working properly. To check that the receiver is operating correctly, place a collar 1ft underneath the receiver (the end opposite the end with the LEDs). If the 1ft LED isn't flashing continuously, change the battery, but if the battery in the receiver is new, change the batteries in the collar.

The transmitter collar is powered by two 393 batteries. Do not use zinc air type batteries. (Other popular equivalent batteries are V393, SR48, RW48, R393/15 and SR48W.) Cold weather conditions have been known to lower the life expectancy of batteries.

To remove the batteries, simply slacken off the collar's strap enough to open up the black transmitter casing. Slide the case open and this will expose the two batteries. Holding the unit, slip off the cover to the right so that the piece with the batteries inserted is on the right-hand side of the housing. The batteries can now be removed and replaced by placing the top battery with the domed terminal (−) facing upwards showing a blue ring around the battery. The lower battery should have the flat face upwards (+). Holding the two parts firmly, slide shut and click into position. With the transmitter functional, wrap some insulating tape around the join and close the strapping tight.

Fit this collar to the ferret, loop the strap over the ferret's neck and tighten. This will require some practice as not every ferret is built with the same shape or size of neck. Test the transmitter with the receiver to ensure that the batteries are live and inserted correctly. Test the collar the same as you would the receiver. If the batteries have been fitted incorrectly just change them over. The transmitting modules are weatherproof, but the battery compartment is only water-resistant, so, in order to protect these parts, a piece of tape inserted around the join is recommended. As with any ferret-finder set, when finished for the day it is recommended that you remove all batteries from the set and place them in a safe, dry place for protection.

Once the batteries have been inserted and you have determined that the system is working, switch the locater receiver box on. Place the search and locate switch on search and hold the receiver flat with the LED end nearest (facing) you. Move into the area where you think the ferret is likely to be. If the pitch of the pips goes down rather than up, this means the distance is getting greater, not nearer. Stop and wave the receiver left and right in an upwards and downwards motion until you find the highest pitch, then follow it. Once you have found the best horizontal direction by moving the device left and right, move closer to the signal until you are 10ft (3m) or less from the ferret. Switch the receiver from search to the locate mode for precise positional location. The receiver goes from being held horizontally to being held vertically, with the LEDs on the top. With a bit of practice you should quickly be over the ferret's position and the red flashing LEDs should give you an estimate of how deep it is. Once directly above or nearest the location of the collar you will find the sweet spot, usually around 1ft (30cm) square. Find the centre of this square to establish the true sweet spot – this is the place to start digging.

The reading is taken from the bottom row of numbers in locate mode and not from the top row as in search mode. The receiver will have these clearly marked on the handset. The bottom numbers go from 1ft to 10ft; remember that these readings may be affected by the soil conditions and are set out as a guide only. Once you have worked an area, you will become accustomed to what the actual working reading depth is. The probe is then used to double-check where the pipe is when you are within a short distance from the ferret's collar. When nearly there, dig carefully and that way the chance of an injury to the ferret is minimal.

THE MK3 FERRET FINDER

Deben had ensured that a suitable replacement was ready for the original Mk1 set before the components' availability stopped. After flirting briefly with the Mk2, the new improved Mk3 was designed, tested and launched in 2005. I personally think that the people at Deben deserve a lot of credit for the manner in which they worked hard, listened to the constructive criticism and produced this new system. Again, I was fortunate enough to be in the privileged position of being one of the first ferreters to test the new Mk3 system in both the factory and the field. After several consultations with Deben regarding the collar fittings and the practicality of the design for use in the field, and then the actual testing itself, I tried my hardest to break it. Faults were found, removed and corrected, but just like any other ferreter, I wanted this system to work properly and be reliable in the field, as my ferrets and work will depend on this equipment functioning correctly and reliably.

When we look closely at the Mk3, you will see many similarities to the way in which the old Mk1 ferret finder worked. The improvements made to the Mk3 reiterate just why many, including myself, prefer to use and endorse the usage of the Mk3 ferret-finder system. It has everything that the earlier models had, plus upgrades and extras. The receiver handset is weatherproof for everyday usage and even though mine has on occasions ended up underwater, they are not designed to be submerged. This is the reason why there is no earpiece fitted to the Mk3 receiver, as this would give the water a passage to the internal workings. The tone of noise emitted from the Mk3 is unique and hard to ignore. This initially upset many users, so Deben then introduced a pinpointer control on the back of the receiver to ensure that the noise could be heard when you wanted it and muted when you didn't. The pinpointer works on the same principle as the dial on the Mk1; it allows a degree of control over the sensitivity and therefore the sounds emitted. The sound of the receiver alters as you home in on the ferret's transmitter collar. As you reduce the sensitivity, the receiver emits sounds only at the range to which you have set the dial. The sensitivity control allows you to mute the sound and only use the flashing red LEDs as a guide to find the collar, enabling the ferreter to use this system in complete silence if required. To ensure a weatherproof receiver, the on/off and locate/search switches are magnetic reed, which in layman's terms means there are no moving parts for the weather's elements to find their way into the internal workings (unlike the Mk1) and also increases reliability.

The range was reduced to 16ft (4.9m) to preserve the life of the batteries. Both of the Mk3's collars have a long battery life due to the change in the manner in which the transmitter works. The improved circuitry in the Mk3 enables its system to detect the signals sent from many Mk3 collars at the same time,

but rejects the interference and rogue signals from elsewhere. It has a search and locate mode that means you can search for your ferrets within a range of 16ft and when you are within 8ft (2.4m) of the signal, you switch from the search to the locate mode. The hand-held receiver goes from being pointed horizontally to being held vertically, reminiscent of the other receivers. This enables the ferreter to confidently locate his ferret to within 6in (15cm). The sweet spot is around 12in (30cm) square; you then locate the centre of this spot to find the true sweet spot. This is the spot at which to start digging. This increased range in the search mode enables you to predict where the ferret is without trampling all over a warren.

The receiver has a series of red flashing LEDs that indicate the distance from the

The versatile Mk3 and collar. (Steven Taylor)

Always ensure that the batteries are fitted correctly. (Steven Taylor)

receiver to the collar, working in tangent with a varying pitch sounder. The LED lights are more distinct and keep within the designated depth reading. This aids the dig and gives you the confidence that you have the sweet spot. There can be variations because of the different soil conditions throughout the UK, the worst being hard substances like rock, chalk and especially wet clay. Whilst using the Mk1, the signal would vary a bit because it was on a wheel, but with a sticker the ambiguity wasn't as noticeable as it is in a specifically numbered flashing LED. The unmistakable tone of these bleeps quickens the closer you get to the collar; if using more than one collar you will hear multiple bleeps.

The battery life for the receiver is around thirty hours and by that I mean thirty working hours – thirty hours of the on switch being on and when worked out this could be

as little as a month, or, for many, the whole season. When the batteries in the Mk3 begin to fade, the LEDs appear to fade and the calibration weakens.

The original Mk3 collars are the same design externally as the Mk2, but are set in grey resin as opposed to black. The strapping has moved with the times and is made from a synthetic material, though the increased width of the strap has caused a bit of a stir, but I have used them on very small to very large ferrets and with the strap customized with a few extra holes to fit the ferrets, I have had no problems with the collar coming off. With the slick, small shape of the transmitter, the collars fit through the nets with the minimum of fuss. The strap length can sometimes cause a bit of a problem, as some ferrets' necks are so large that the collar doesn't fit properly. If this is the case, Deben stocks the larger collars for the terrier finder and, with a little trim, this problem is overcome. However, when fitting on leaner ferrets, the spare length of collar sticks up in the air, giving an object that could disturb the net. I fit a small elastic band on the collar and tuck the spare webbing underneath. With the new webbing, you do not have the possibility of the collar weakening and snapping like an untreated leather collar, or the end expanding and making it hard to buckle. If you do cut or put on a new strap, I always heat a spoon and smooth the edge of the collar so that it doesn't fray in time and make tightening the buckle a nightmare.

However, on the Mk3M collar (the latest version of the Mk3, so called because it is switched on and off with a magnet), Deben has reverted to the natural leather collar that was used on the Mk1 sets and the transmitter housing has a screw top as opposed to the earlier model clip mechanism, so once the battery is in, it stays in. The batteries are then turned on and off with a magnet housed at the base of the receiver. To check if your receiver has a magnet fitted, the unit will have an arrow with a dot mould pointing downwards. If using a model without a magnet or you are using a Mk1 receiver with the improved collars, a magnet is supplied with each new transmitter collar purchased. One of the weaknesses on the original Mk3 transmitter housing on the collar was that the little plastic snap hooks sometimes broke.

Again, I fitted insulating tape to protect the housing on the earlier Mk3 collar, because I found that small pieces of dirt, sand and soil crept under the collar cover throughout the day and could move the contact away from the battery. I would strongly advise all those with these collars to tape the collar up before commencing to ferret. I know many don't bother, but for the sake of a little bit of tape you can ensure no slip-ups are going to happen when wanting to find your ferret and rabbit. With the improvements made with the new Mk3M collar, a screw cap ensures total protection especially from water; the need for tape has been made obsolete.

Mk3 Ferret Finder Operating Instructions

As with all ferret finder systems, if you notice that the operating range is reducing and/or the pulse speed slowing down, change the batteries in the transmitter (collar). If you are using the original version of the Mk3 with a clip-shut collar, ensure that the battery compartment is not only clean but dry as well. To obtain extra protection, place some insulating tape around the joins on the collar's housing. A 9V PP3 battery powers all versions of the ferret-finder receivers. Rechargeable batteries can be used for the receivers, but, as with all batteries, once the power starts to reduce, the receiver will produce a less accurate reading.

Remove the battery cover on the rear of the unit and insert a new battery as shown by the diagram on the inside of the battery housing. Once replaced and the battery cover is back on, the receiver can then be checked to see if it is working properly. To check that the receiver is operating correctly, place a collar 0.5ft (15cm) underneath the receiver (opposite to the end with the LEDs). If the 0.5ft LED isn't flashing continuously, change the battery, but if the battery is new, change the batteries in the collar.

The Mk3 transmitter collar is powered by two 393 batteries. Do not use zinc air type batteries. (Other popular equivalent batteries are V393, SR48, RW48, R393/15 and SR48W.) Cold weather conditions have been known to lower the life expectancy of batteries. The Mk3M collar is powered by two 394 batteries.

To remove the batteries from the collar, simply slacken off the collar's strap enough to open up the transmitter casing. Slide the case open and this will expose the two batteries. If you hold the case so that the piece with the batteries inserted is on the right-hand side, the batteries can be removed and replaced by placing the top battery in with the domed terminal (–) facing upwards, showing a blue ring around the battery. The bottom battery should have the flat face upwards

Fitting the collar. (Steven Taylor)

(+). Holding the two parts firmly, slide shut and click into position. With the transmitter functional, wrap some insulating tape around the join and close the strapping tight.

To correctly fit this collar to the ferret, simply add a few holes in the collar to fit your ferret's neck, then loop the strap over the ferret's neck and tighten. To check if it is on correctly, try to pull the collar over the head of the ferret and turn the whole collar 360 degrees. If the collar is loose, it will come off; if it is too tight, you will not be able to turn it in a full circle. This will require some practice as not every ferret is built with the same shape or size of neck. Test the transmitter with the receiver to ensure that the batteries are live and inserted correctly. Test the collar the same as you would the receiver. If the batteries have been fitted incorrectly, just change them over. The early Mk3 collar's

transmitting modules are not completely weatherproof, so to protect these parts a piece of tape wrapped around the join is recommended.

In the Mk3M, the batteries are inserted into the module by removing the leather strap and then unscrewing the lid and placing the two batteries on top of each other. The lid is then screwed back on finger tight and the whole compartment is fully waterproof. You will not need to open up this module until a new set of batteries is required. To switch the Mk3M on and off you use the magnet inserted on the bottom of the Mk3 receiver set. The sets fitted with a magnet are marked by an arrow and dot on the bottom end of the receiver. If you use an earlier model, it will not have a magnet fitted so therefore there will be no arrow and dot moulded onto the receiver, but to counteract this, in every new collar's packaging is a little magnet in order to be able to use this collar with your receiver.

As with the Mk1, 2 and 3 (with the grey clip module as opposed to the screw-top version of the Mk3M), it is recommended to remove all batteries from the set and place them in a safe, dry tub for protection. To clean any soil or dirt from the collar if any were to get inside, simply wash clean with warm water and dry thoroughly to ensure the system's terminals are clean and bright. The compartment must be dry before use.

Working the Mk3 set isn't a million miles away from using the older Mk1 version. Once the batteries have been inserted and you have determined that the system is working, switch on the locater receiver box. Place the search and locate switch on search and hold the receiver flat (see diagram) with the LED end nearest (facing) you. Move into the area you think the ferret is likely to be. If the pitch of the pips goes down rather than up, the distance is getting greater, not nearer. Stop and wave the receiver left and right in an upwards

and downwards motion until you find the highest pitch, then follow it. If you want to search/locate in silence, on the sets fitted with a pinpointer control you can turn the volume down so that it only sounds at a particular depth, or not at all. Once you have found the best horizontal direction by moving from left to right, and if not working in really deep warrens, move until you are less than 8ft (2.4m) from the ferret (if that is possible). Rotate the receiver and switch from search to locate, point the receiver to the ground (see diagram) and move it to obtain the highest pitch. With a bit of practice, you should now be over the ferret's position and the red flashing LEDs should give you an estimate of how deep it is. With the ferret finder models fitted with the pin pointer control, you can control the sensitivity of the pitch sounder as you approach the collar, allowing you to reduce the sensitivity so the receiver emits sounds only at a set range. You can also use this control to mute the receiver altogether whilst still using the LED display – this enables you to work in complete silence.

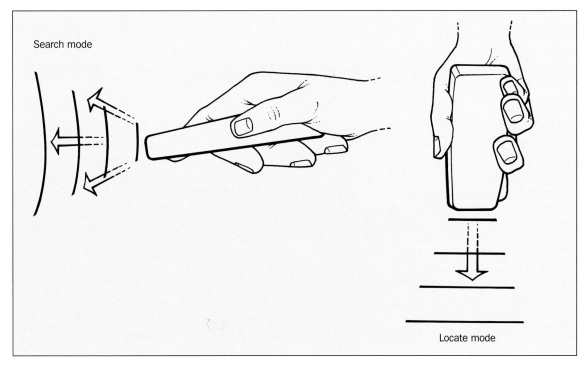

How to hold a receiver in the search and locate mode.

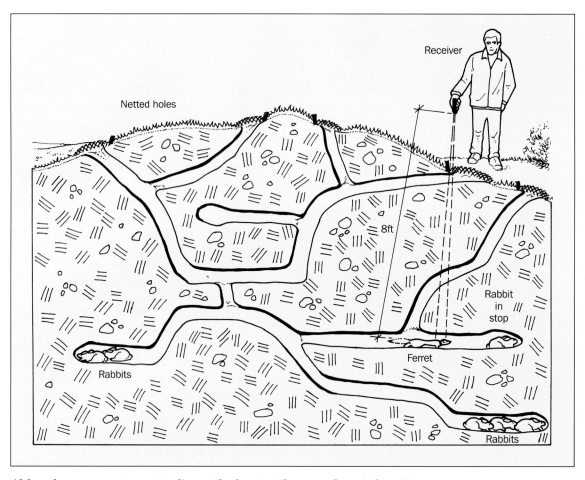

Netted holes

Receiver

8ft

Rabbit
in
stop

Ferret

Rabbits

Rabbits

Although you may not want to dig out the ferret, at least you know where it is.

Whilst on the search mode, the receiver will detect the transmitter up to approximately 16ft (5m) away. The LED dots under the set depths on the face show the distance between receiver and transmitter. A set pitch or bleep enables you to hear the change in reading, but it is the numbered reading that you will check from. Once less than 8ft (2.4m) away, switch the set to the locate mode for precise positional location. Move towards the signal, again following the strongest signal's route until directly above or nearest the location of the collar, as these sets work three dimensionally. The locate reading is taken from the bottom row of numbers and not the top row as in search mode. The receiver will have these clearly marked on the handset. The bottom

numbers go from 0.5ft (15cm) to 8ft; these readings are affected by the soil conditions and the numbers are set out as a guide only. Once you have worked an area, you will become accustomed to the actual working reading depth. These readings are only used as a guide; the guide set out by Deben is just an estimation. One point to remember when using this guide is to take into account the space between the collar on the bottom of the rabbit burrow and the measurement to the top of the pipe to which you are digging. The reading may say 32in (80cm) but the pipe may be 8in (20cm), so the distance to the pipe will be only 24in (60cm) (see diagram opposite). This is why, when I am within a short distance of the ferret, I keep checking to see where the ferret is

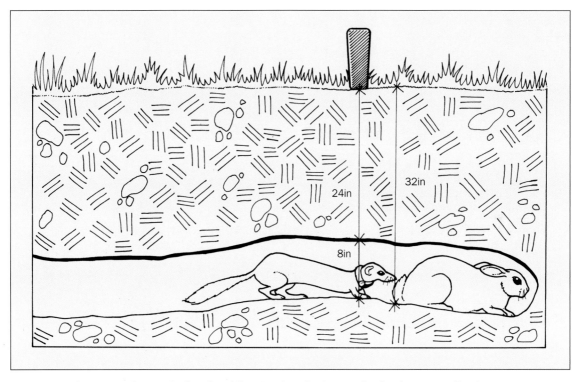

It is easy to forget to subtract the height of the pipe in calculating the depth you are digging.

and if it has moved. The probe is then used to double-check where the pipe is and when I am nearly there, I dig carefully. If all goes according to plan, the ferret should appear and you can pull the rabbit or rabbits out.

The alternative for those ferreters who find the search and locate mode confusing is to use the system on locate only, proceeding exactly as with the old Mk1 system.

Some Tips on Using the Ferret Finder

If you are ferreting solo or a larger/new warren, it can be beneficial to tape a receiver box (switched on) to a long net pole and place it at the furthest point to which you want the ferrets to travel or you can safely see. This ensures that you get a signal when the ferrets are reaching their or your furthest point. This will reassure you that no ferrets have sneaked off and gone freelance hunting.

Whichever ferret finder system you use, always ensure that it works consistently and

correctly. Always carry some spare batteries just in case. If the unthinkable happens and the set breaks down, ensure that you have a fail-safe alternative method of retrieving and removing your ferret/ferrets safely. If using the Mk3M collars, ensure that the collar is switched on before entering your ferrets. It can be easy to get into the habit of switching the collar off while still on the ferret, then forgetting to switch it back on. To be safe, only switch off the collar when it is off the ferret.

QUIRKY METHODS OF RETRIEVAL

There are several other methods of retrieval that people use, but I find these to be a bit haphazard and not as consistent as using a ferret finder. The first is the age-old method of squeaking, calling, jangling keys or tapping the mouth of the rabbit hole. The ferrets are used to hearing your sound at feeding time whilst at home and get accustomed to

Place a ferret finder (switched on) on the boundary of where you are working, to alert you to any ferrets that have slipped your attention.

associating this sound with food. However, when out in the field, this method only stands a chance of working if your ferret is free to move away from a rabbit and do you really want your ferrets to ignore a rabbit in the first place? If the ferret has killed a rabbit and is trapped behind it, this method becomes seriously flawed.

A well-practised trick to get a stubborn ferret back to the surface is to slit open the stomach of a freshly killed rabbit and blow or allow the natural wind to carry the scent underground. The aroma of the fresh intestine triggers the ferret's primitive curiosity and its hunting instinct kicks in. While I have used this method on many occasions, I have found it to have two serious weaknesses. Firstly, you need to have a freshly killed rabbit and this isn't always available, especially if you have just started ferreting early that morning. The other is that if the ferret is determined or trapped, the only way that ferret will surface is if it is in your hand after you have dug it out.

A TRAP BOX

A trap box is a box that is placed inside a well-used entrance in the general area that the ferret was last seen. The other holes of the warren are filled in. Warm bedding and a piece of fresh meat are placed inside the trap. The meat lures the ferret into the box and once it has entered the box, it stands on a treddle and the trap door closes behind it. The ferret is trapped, but is also safe not only from predators and traps designed for pests, but also from walking off again after a fresh scent. Some ferreters put a normal carrying box at the entrance of the warren in a similar fashion, with warm bedding and food inside the open box and many ferrets have been recovered this way, although I view this as a rather lazy method of ferret retrieval, in particular as it will not recover a trapped ferret. It goes with saying that to many ferreters, their ferrets are the most prized members of the ferreting team and they will do all in their power to recover them.

CHAPTER SIX

Working Your Ferrets

Traditionally, ferreting has always been practised in the months with an 'r' in them, that is, September until April. However, the change in our climate and the resulting change in nature's mechanics have meant that we will have to adapt in the same manner as nature has. We need to wake up to the sobering fact that our weather during autumn, winter and spring is never going to return to what it once was and accept that one day we will be able to ferret, in one way or another, the whole year round.

My own ferreting doesn't start until October, but it is November before any serious ferreting is practised. The season finishes around April, although summer jobs are taken on if I can ferret them to my satisfaction. In the early parts of the season, a large tract of the land on which I hunt is used for shooting. I am therefore limited in the places I can go and the boundaries I can cross, although I have permission from the farmer or gamekeeper to work the hedgerows and places well away from the game covers. These are done as soon as I can and not too close to shoot days. It pays to work with the shoot rather than antagonize it. However, ignorance is rife amongst a lot of folk, and not just from outside the ferreting community, as to what ferreting really is and the good it does the landscape. On these shooting grounds, once

the first day of February arrives, speed is of the essence, as the greenery will be starting to grow back and hampering the ferreter's work. This just complicates the job of bolting or trying to bolt rabbits that have paired up or are already pregnant.

It is not just the outlook of when to ferret that has changed, but also how we ferret and with what equipment. Modern farming techniques dictate the lay of the land in certain calendar months, but more importantly at what stage the crops are in their growth. To protect these crops, it is best to get at the rabbits before the crops start their growth spurts. Before we embark on any day's ferreting, it is wise to just run through a mental risk assessment. I know someday the bureaucrats will want us to wear protective clothing for everything, but a personal risk assessment just takes a few minutes and it will ensure you haven't overlooked any possible escape route. Mentally running through where you are going ferreting, how many ferrets you will need, what nets, how many and where they are to be placed could highlight any hidden dangers to you or your animals and the impending bag. You must decide when the last ferrets are to be put to ground, giving them enough time to work in case of failing light, and also whether you have to notify anybody of your whereabouts and at

Summertime ferreting. (Author)

roughly what time you will return. Plenty of ferreters ferret solo, so if you are in a secluded area, it is wise to let someone know where you are just in case you put your foot down a rabbit hole and break your ankle and are unable to move. It pays always to carry a mobile phone with good coverage.

In Chapter 2, we saw that the rabbit now breeds nearly all year round, spending the summer recolonizing the land to ensure further ferreting trips are required in order to keep the rabbit population under control. Once you can get to the warrens, you can start ferreting; this may be August or it may be as late as November, but unless you can see what you are doing there is no point start-

OPPOSITE: The warmer climate means a different approach to ferreting clothing. (Steven Taylor)

ing ferreting. It is pointless having as many escapees as caught rabbits. Once the land is clear, the rabbits will be there for the taking. Whether ferreting for a few hours' sport or for pest-control purposes (the difference has been outlined in Chapter 3), the difference is in the mind, actions and expectations, not only in the results. By setting out a game plan, tackling the harder parts first and not expecting a high number of easily reached or caught rabbits, you can gain maximum results, be it for a full day, or for a few hours, an early finish and a quick pint at the local hostelry.

I have found that it pays to plan any outing in advance, because although you may see a lot of rabbits in a certain field, it doesn't necessarily mean that they are living there. By locating the areas of damage and also the areas that require a bit of cover cutting back, you should expose the places that need to be ferreted. But be warned, serious clearance can move the rabbits on to another area if they feel insecure with the safety of their cover gone. By planning the day ahead, you can start on the bigger, more daunting warrens, which are usually found around the area with the most rabbit damage. Ferreting these areas first will give the damaged crop a greater chance of recovery if caught early enough. The main bulk of the rabbits should be here, so it makes more sense to start with these warrens to give you ample time to ferret them. These are not warrens to start ferreting with only an hour or two of daylight left. The rabbits in the smaller warrens and the warrens themselves can be ferreted a lot quicker at the latter part of the day with failing light. Better results can be gained with consecutive days of ferreting, as the rabbits have nowhere to hide. It is likely that if you leave it a week or two before returning, the main bulk of the warrens will have been repopulated, meaning that you are back at square one.

Let's take it for granted that you want to tackle a big, established warren, so time to start planning. Large warrens deserve a bit more respect. Don't be afraid to tackle these warrens, they may not be as daunting as they first appear, but ask for help if you think you will need it. Mentally break down the larger warrens into smaller ones by placing your help around the warren in equal gaps. With the extra eyes and hands, most of the larger warrens will be easier to ferret, making the smaller warrens feel harder in comparison as you will be by yourself. Remember, if you are to return at a later date, do not expect the good work you did previously to be the same, unless you are returning the next day.

It is not only the ferrets that will decide on your success but the nets and netting you use. Use the wrong nets in the wrong situation and you are in big trouble. Do you just use long nets to divide and encircle the area and risk hole-hoppers, do you lay purse net over the whole area if possible, or do you combine the two?

If you split up the larger warrens with stop nets, if the rabbits do hole-hop just start laying a few nets. The rabbits already know something is up so a little more annoyance and disturbance isn't going to do any more damage. With nets and humans, space them out at regular intervals and give them a certain space to keep; let the ferrets move freely but the humans should stay within their allocated areas. The more relaxed your outlook of a warren, the calmer and more efficient it should be to ferret, although you should never be afraid to alter your tactics whilst the ferrets are down working.

The day's ferreting will not always go to plan. I am always amazed by the amount of people who have said that you have to take the good with the bad days whilst ferreting, but we never read about these bad day in books and magazine articles. This has made me wonder why, as I would have thought that accounts of a truly bad day would be just as important as the good days when written down for records and historical reasons. Without them, we simply paint a false picture. Also, it makes you appreciate the good days more after you have had a bad one.

Bad days do happen, usually at a time when you least want them to. One such day happened to me and this can be typical of how your week can go sometimes. The date in the diary said I was due to ferret a cemetery in Norfolk as they were experiencing problems with the rabbits eating the flowers on the graves. The area had been cleared of undergrowth by the church warden, as it had resembled a jungle, and I was keen to make a start, as the greenery regrows at an alarming rate and the last thing I wanted to have to deal with was a covering of sharp new stingers. The whole of the UK at this time also appeared to be experiencing an outbreak of myxomatosis. With the warmer winters, the midges, mosquitoes and fleas are having a field day spreading this disease. The bank I was about to ferret was about 76yd (70m) in length and had a ditch before the next bank

Take your time to lay the nets. (Steven Taylor)

to stop our illegal hosts of the human species from camping behind the cemetery, so if digging was called for, the ground shouldn't be too compact, just deep.

A lot of work and effort had been put into this job with the clearance, the netting and the time spent organizing the day on which I could work, just for the scourge of myxomatosis to raise its head again. The problem with ferreting myxyed rabbits is that they do not have the inclination or energy to bolt, but the dog still marks their presence. When the ferrets are entered, they simply go in for the kill and move on. I can understand why some less experienced ferreters would start to doubt themselves, the dog and ferret, for there is no visible end result. This isn't your purist's idea of ferreting but when it is pest control, a dead rabbit is a dead rabbit, and at least their suffering will be over. It amazes me just how quickly myxomatosis spreads through our countryside but each year the rabbit population recovers just as quickly as in previous years.

The winter can get tiresome with too much digging and when you finally break through to reach the rabbit and you are greeted by twenty or so flies escaping to find another meal, it can get disheartening. The only positive aspect to a situation like this is that myxomatosis has already killed all of the rabbits, and therefore there are no rabbits left to cause any damage. Days like this are a part and parcel of the job, but when ferreting for financial gain, the pressure and stress levels can go up a lot. It isn't just the rabbits that you are working to trying to reduce; you are also trying to maintain and improve your working reputation, as nothing sounds better than a recommendation from a satisfied customer.

DECISION TIME: NETS, GUNS, DOG OR HAWK?

The ferret doesn't work for us – it works for itself. Our job is to clean, feed and transport this animal about, but our main priority is to decide what to use, where to use it and when. If you want to bolt a few rabbits for your dog or hawk, the equipment required will be far less than if you decide to net. Shooting over the ferrets can be a serious method of control if enough guns can be present to shoot the bolted rabbits. We owe it to the ferret for the extremely hard graft it does day in and day out that we do our job correctly; that is, lay the nets properly and ensure there is no slip-up when the rabbit obliges and bolts. Nothing is more frustrating than the sight of sloppily laid nets, or, worse still, sloppily laid and sloppily made nets, especially in the case of using the wrong net for the wrong position.

FERRETING ALONE OR WITH HELP?

Some, like myself, have very little choice in the matter. I live in an area where there are very few reliable ferreters and the few I do

OPPOSITE: The travelling box. (Steven Taylor)

know all lead normal lives with normal jobs, so midweek help is normally out of the question. Even on the paid jobs that I have priced for more than one ferreter, I struggle to get reliable and trustworthy help. On the bigger, more difficult warrens, I will try to ferret these at a weekend or over a holiday so that I can get up to five people to help me ferret. I do enjoy ferreting alone with just my dogs, ferrets and the rabbits for company, but it is the warrens that dictate whether or not I need help.

GETTING THE FERRETS BOXED AND PREPARED FOR THEIR JOURNEY

The day starts with getting the ferrets ready for the journey to your ground. Before the ferrets can go into their travelling boxes, the boxes themselves must be ready. There should be fresh straw or a bedding of your choice, plus shavings on the floor to soak up any urine or droppings that will occur during the coming hours spent inside the box. Cleaning these boxes out on your return is a good routine to get into, because if the day was wet or muddy the ferrets will want a clean and warm box for their next outing, not a wet, dirty-smelling box that may harbour some ticks or fleas gained from the rabbits or warrens they have just worked.

Decide how many ferrets you need, how many boxes and which ferrets go into what boxes. If two ferrets don't get along, avoid putting them together in a confined space, as there are few things more irritating when driving than the smell and sound of bickering ferrets. Usually one of my own bowback boxes (*see* Chapter 4) will carry five jills or three hobs comfortably; otherwise, I have built a special travelling box in which I can carry a dozen ferrets in comfort. Although small enough not to take up all the room in the car, it is large enough to give the ferrets room to do natural things in the corner and not on top of each other. If carried properly, the ferrets will be fresh and raring to go when

Even the most docile of animals can be dangerous. (Steven Taylor)

you finally open the lid and prepare them for the work ahead, rather than stretching their cramped bodies back into shape and thus wasting valuable ferreting time.

It may be possible to collar up your ferrets with the ferret finders before you leave the warmth of the shed or house, but if you have a good drive ahead, it is surprising just how many hours of the battery life can be wasted this way. I always collar up while I am letting the ground settle after the nets have been laid, or while having a quick cup of tea before starting to ferret. On the days that a larger warren is to be worked and I have help, I collar up all the ferrets, sometimes up to a dozen, so that whenever anybody goes for a ferret, it has a collar on. I have witnessed countless ferrets being put down a hole without a collar on, even by some experienced ferreters, as on the spur of the moment their mind is on other things. It is always better to be safe than sorry. In Chapter 5, you will find a step-by-step guide to the placing and removal of ferret collars, whether using a Mk1, 2 or 3 Deben ferret finder. I simply cannot understand why people still ferret without the use of a ferret finder set and I wouldn't recommend ferreting without one fitted to each ferret worked. With the ferrets now collared-up, you are ready for action.

APPROACHING THE WARRENS AND THE USE OF FIELD CRAFT

Approaching the warren cannot always be done in a silent manner, or with the wind blowing your scent away rather than down the holes. Always conduct yourself as quietly as possible and take into consideration the noise and vibrations made whilst netting up. Let the ground settle before entering your ferrets. Look to your dog for guidance, especially when you are ferreting woodland and the wind has blown loads of old, dead crispy leaves into the holes, making the warren appear vacant, but if the dog says otherwise, then the warren needs to be ferreted. These warrens are often overlooked, but are usually the best places to ferret. Try to be as observant as possible when looking for the bolt-holes, otherwise the leaves will explode and a white tail will be waving you farewell.

ARE THERE ANY HIDDEN DANGERS?

The dangers that may face you and your ferrets might not necessarily be the obvious ones. Wasps like to build their nests in resident rabbit warrens just as much as disused ones. Other hidden animals that may concern you are rats – they usually bolt from a rabbit warren if they aren't defending any young and as the pipes are larger, they can easily move past the ferret. Snakes often rest during the summer and autumn in shallow warrens, especially on heath or woodland. Foxes, especially a small vixen, can slip into almost any warren for a quick rest without too much trouble and could cause injury to your ferrets. You also need to check whether there are any animals in the vicinity that may pose a risk to you or your dog/ferrets, such as a bull, bullocks, horses or farm dogs. Also keep an eye out for farm machinery being used or moved. It always pays to think of these things, as when they do pop up at least you will be better prepared.

SHOOTING OVER FERRETS

Whatever you are getting up to on the surface, the way in which the ferret works above and below ground is exactly the same. It is how the rabbits are stopped or caught above the ground which now interests us. We are no longer talking about nets, we are talking about shotguns, which, if not used in a correct manner, will not only stop the rabbit, but your ferrets and possibly you as well. Careful consideration must be given towards those who are going to be pulling the trigger; a net is forgiving, 32g of lead isn't!

Nothing gets the blood pumping and the adrenalin flowing more than the sight of bolting rabbits, but this is no place for people who are inexperienced guns. It is possible to nurture a gun, one in at a time, with careful, considerate and safe guns around them to give the benefit of their experience to the newcomer. Shooting over ferrets has the potential to go horrendously wrong, as shotguns may not only kill the rabbit or an unlucky ferret, but also a human if safety isn't taken seriously. I have seen that famous Cornish countryman, Chris Green, and his displays hundreds of times. The man is bang on (pardon the pun) when it comes to appreciating gun safety. During his demonstration, he tells us how he was made aware of how dangerous a gun can be. He props his gun up in the centre of the arena, stands motionless with his arms crossed and stares at the gun intensely. As he stands back, the crowd, unaware of what he is doing, waits intently for something exciting to happen. After about thirty seconds he then goes and collects the gun, pointing out that by itself the gun is harmless, it is only when a human is let loose near one that it can become potentially lethal.

I used to do a lot of rabbit shooting, but nowadays I prefer the quiet life. However, the best shooting day to date was when I was ferret boy for a team of three crack shots who all knew how to shoot rabbits. I learnt a lot from that day. We got forty-nine rabbits, a total only bettered once in nineteen years in my

area. Preparation is vital, as you must have a clear plan of action in your head, the same as you need when ferreting with nets, dogs or hawks. You must know where the warrens start and finish, the direction of possible bolts and hazards that may hinder the guns, whether it be stock, the weather or the foliage around the warrens. Sometimes, the rabbit will try to creep out of the warren, rather than bolt out at a rate of knots, especially when the bolt-hole is amongst undergrowth, though sometimes even with guns a-blazing, they bolt a dream. If you have the luxury of a reconnaissance mission a week or two in advance, you may be able to clear any troublesome bushes or ask for some machinery to be moved or stock housed, but, in reality, this is not usually possible, so most ferreters have to learn to work around the obstacles.

When I am the ferret boy for a team of guns, I usually use my friends whom I know and whose shooting I can trust. Any newcomers are tested with a few easy days just to run my eye over them to see if they will fit in. Everybody must be at ease with each other, as well as being a good rabbit shot. Rabbit shooting is possibly one of the hardest disciplines, as it may be all snap shooting or those horrible long mazy runs that let you think too long and, if you are like me, miss. Once the rabbit has bolted, there may only be a few seconds' worth of visibility before they run into cover. If you have thought ahead, you will have made a mental note of where the cover has a gap, hopefully giving you a second chance if needed.

The manner in which the rabbit reacts to the sound of a gun isn't always what you would expect. Unless the rabbit has been shot over before, the sound of a shotgun will be completely alien to it – and if a rabbit hasn't experienced the dangers that a gun poses, how is it meant to know of its dangers? You would imagine that the rabbit, because of its hearing range, would be more alarmed

OPPOSITE: Confidence, concentration and trust are required when guns are involved. (Steven Taylor)

by the sound of the gun than a pair of size nines tramping above the ground, but rabbits are more alarmed by vibrations than airborne noise. However, noise or not, the ferret will need to give the rabbit some encouragement to bolt in order for you to have a chance of a shot. On many occasions, the rabbit will not bolt and will be prepared to face the ferret, or it will sit it out in a stop end until the danger has passed rather than bolt above ground if it has any doubts about its safety. If a rabbit has bolted and then goes down another hole, if it realizes what is happening it will be as stubborn as a mule to bolt again and more often than not it will require a bit of spadework to get the rabbit out.

Just as when ferreting with nets, the size of the warren will dictate how many ferrets are used, but you must decide how many guns you can safely use and how much time you should give to the ferrets in working each warren. I always try to work the ferrets and leave the bulk of the shooting to others, although on rare occasions I have my gun ready, especially if there are only a couple of us. However, I know that as soon as I put the gun down to pick up a ferret or rabbit, another will bolt out and escape. When ferreting with guns, safety is of paramount importance and that is why I mainly only ferret, so that I can concentrate fully on the ferrets. The rabbits have a habit of hole-hopping, but when you become tuned into shooting rabbits, a large percentage of these rabbits will not make the holes again, as they pause for a millisecond and that is enough time for the guns to shoot the rabbit, as long as it isn't directly in front of a hole. When the rabbit surfaces to bolt, if it stops for that millisecond to test the air for danger, there can be no ferret in hot pursuit, otherwise it wouldn't have stopped. If, on the other hand, it bolts straight out, the ferret is near and this is a lesson the guns that shoot for me know all too well. Shooting a rabbit directly in front of its entrance/exit hole will result in a dead or injured rabbit being forced down the hole for the ferret to meet and another possible lay up, or, worse, a frightened or injured ferret.

133

A purist shooting rabbits would wait until the rabbit is well away from the warren before pulling the trigger, but, in realistic terms, this would mean a lot of escaped rabbits as the trees and hedging offer a protective barrier for the rabbit to hide behind. The team I use are amongst the finest team of guns I have ever seen shoot rabbits, and that is a statement I do not make lightly. We use two, three or four guns at any one time; the terrain we shoot ranged from thick hedges and ditches to open land with every combination in-between. The team knows how highly I rate safety, for them, me and especially for my ferrets. They understand why I mope when they start to miss and count the rabbits missed as opposed to the hits. Credit is always given where credit is due, the same as a little constructive criticism where needed. When ferreting a dubious area that is not really suitable for shooting, I lay a small stop net to avoid any possible escapees, but, as with all aspects of shooting, if you deem the shot safe, go for it. Hesitation can cause more problems, because when you have a hesitant gun, more rabbits escape than should. That said, of course it is better to be safe and hesitant than foolhardy and reckless with something as potentially lethal as a gun.

The type of guns used for shooting rabbits varies from the .410, 20 or 12 bore of various designs, be it normal, silenced, double or single barrelled. I prefer the 12 bore, but have been impressed with the smaller 20 bore, as the distance normally shot can be from extreme close range up to the range of 35yd (32m). The sizes of shot that are usually used are a size 6, though for heavier cover, a good 5 shot has the ability to stop the rabbit, even through dense undergrowth.

SETTING THE NETS AND BACK-NETTING

Whether shooting, bolting to the dog or hawk, or netting, the same principles and pointers must be observed. All animals must be broken to ferrets, stood out of direct view of the possible bolting rabbits and all rabbits dispatched as humanely and efficiently as possible. The resulting catch may be high when a proficient dog is used, but the chances of escapees are still high as two may bolt at once. Even when using purse nets, on many occasions when a rabbit has bolted and got itself caught in the net another will run over the pursed rabbit to freedom before the ferreter or dog can reach the net and either guard the open hole or relay a fresh purse net. For this reason alone many use stop or long nets as well.

Each warren is unique, but at the same time they are all essentially equal, consisting of a series of holes, some hidden, some open, some large and some small, all arranged in such a way that the advantage is given to the resident rabbits. It is the job of the ferreter to change that advantage with the use of nets. Laying the purse or poke nets over the entrance and exit holes will go a long way, but when your terrain is full of thorny bushes and inhospitable areas, the long net comes into its own.

As described in Chapter 4, the purse net can only be put over the holes or occasionally over a run, whereas long nets can be placed in a wide variety of positions as dictated to by the terrain. Use them right and the minimum can be used to great effect; get their position wrong and the time spent laying them should act as a lesson to be learnt. You could have the best-made nets in the world, but if you don't learn where to lay them correctly a lot of rabbits will escape. A modern trend amongst ferreters is to use long nets to encircle an area in preference to taking your time and setting purse nets, but this can be a recipe for disaster. The percentage of rabbits hole-hopping will be greater, especially if they know you are there. The long net is a wonderful tool, but it is never going to replace the purse net completely as both nets have a time and a place to be used.

You could use a little stop net through the hedge, surround the lot, or a combination of

OPPOSITE: Laying the nets. (Steven Taylor)

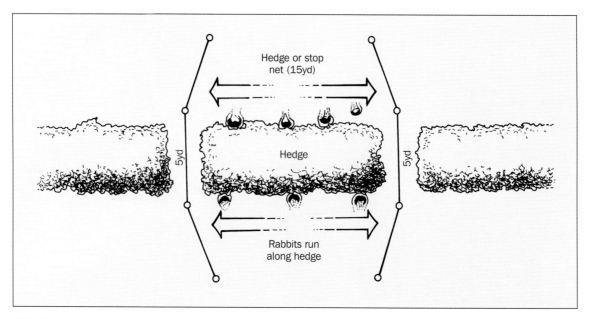

Hedge or stop
net (15yd)

5yd

Hedge

5yd

Rabbits run
along hedge

The placement of hedge or stop nets.

both. As the diagram shows, the area and behaviour of the rabbits will dictate where and how you lay your nets. Once you have ferreted a warren a few times you will be able to second-guess the rabbits' escape routes to great effect. A 5yd (4.5m) or 10yd (9m) net in the right place through a hedge or over a gap in a fence will always catch more than a 105yd (96m) net set in the wrong place.

It pays to net up several warrens before you start ferreting. Firstly, this lets any noise and disturbance settle down before you enter the ferrets. Not only do you save time by being able to move from one netted up warren to another, but, secondly and more importantly, if any rabbits escape, then the warrens just ferreted and about to be ferreted will be covered by nets. Rabbits may be back-netted this way as they try to disappear back down a hole and the net still purses, not outwards but backwards into the hole, hence the term back-netted.

The best way to lay a purse net is to ensure that the net is laid over the hole in a manner that will capture any rabbit coming out at any speed. Ensure the holes are free from twigs and other debris that may inhibit the actions

of the net, especially if the area has been cut back. Place the lower ring (the one opposite to the end with the peg attached) just inside the mouth of the hole; some press the bottom ring into the ground for extra friction. Spread the net out so that it comfortably covers the actual hole and not the whole of the bank as the rabbit should appear from the hole, not from the earth surrounding it. The spare netting in the middle of the net will be needed for holding the pursed rabbit. Nets that are shaped but are too small will simply let the occupant roll out. Once you have ensured the bagging is in the middle of the net, stretch the draw cord that outlines the net and is attached to a peg, then insert the peg into the ground. A common mistake is to have too much slack in the length of draw cord between the peg and the top ring/slider. If this occurs, the net can and will travel some distance before it has been ground to a halt and thus starts to purse. Some peg the net first and then set it, but how can you gauge the draw cord if the net hasn't been set?

OPPOSITE: *Using natural resources to ensure the net lies correctly in a vertical position. (Steven Taylor)*

It is always best to take your time when setting nets, because if you rush things you will start to get sloppy and miss holes, set nets incorrectly, or leave a load of debris in the holes. Not all purse/poke nets will be laid in the conventional way, that is, horizontally. Many holes are in steep inclines or around tree stumps, so you must be capable of keeping the net upright. To stop the net from falling down, push either some small twigs or a few golf tees into the surrounding earth to form leverage for the net to hold onto, thus preventing it sliding down.

UNUSUAL SITUATIONS AND AWKWARD SPOTS

From time to time, you will ferret a truly awkward warren in relation to its location or situation. The rabbit will take up residence anywhere where it feels safe, from the middle of a roundabout, underneath buildings and next to busy shopping centres or sports pavilions. The most difficult situation I have ferreted to date was in the middle of a busy hospital, ferreting underneath the portable operating theatres as they operated. The most flamboyant ferreting was the warrens alongside a busy sports centre. The rabbits were damaging an expensive athletic track and football pitch, but were residing in a bank directly next to the centre. The public was always roaming about, as the centre was open from first light until last light and beyond. Cheekily, the warren was ferreted by adapting to the surroundings. Instead of the usual ferreting clothing we donned a boiler suit, hi-vis vest, hat in order to pass for workmen and laid a load of brooms, rakes and cutting equipment around the bushes. The entire warren was surrounded by a long net. The holes were purse-netted to try to avoid any rabbit hitting the long net, which was placed more as a safety barrier than a net.

OPPOSITE: A true predator will blend into any surrounding in order to catch its prey. (Steven Taylor)

Because the public was used to seeing workmen, they didn't give us a second glance, the bank was ferreted and the rabbits immediately placed inside a plastic fertilizer bag and then off to the vehicle, another example of blending into your surroundings to get a job done.

Many warrens will be in thick, inhospitable hedging where it may be difficult to lay a purse net and you may not have the yardage of long nets to surround the whole area. The best option it to place a small long net through the hedge. The cover of a hedge is where the rabbits feel safe and so they will try to creep out through the dense cover, or they may decide to run. Whatever they do, make sure you have a net waiting. By spotting the rabbit runs and placing a purse net over them, you can watch as the rabbit follows its favoured path and is then caught in the purse net laid over that regularly used hole. However, be warned, if the rabbit isn't under pressure, it will have time to survey its surroundings and I have on more than one occasion experienced rabbits running aside a white or lightly coloured net, either long or hedge.

ENTERING THE FERRETS

When entering your ferrets, take a moment to decide where to use any particular ferret. Don't overuse a favourite; equal out the workload. Do not use a proven killer, or one that will stay in spots that are inaccessible as you will be courting disaster. This is, of course, different to using a ferret that will kill if given the opportunity and then move on. Often these ferrets are valuable members of the team.

Warrens come in all shapes and sizes, from a small one or two hole set, right up to an enormous excavation of over 100yd (91m) in length. Sometimes it can be harder to get the rabbits to bolt in warrens that have fewer entrance and exit holes but a large amount of piping under the surface. In these deceiving places, the rabbits become masters at running rings around the ferrets. These warrens

Entering the ferret. (Steven Taylor)

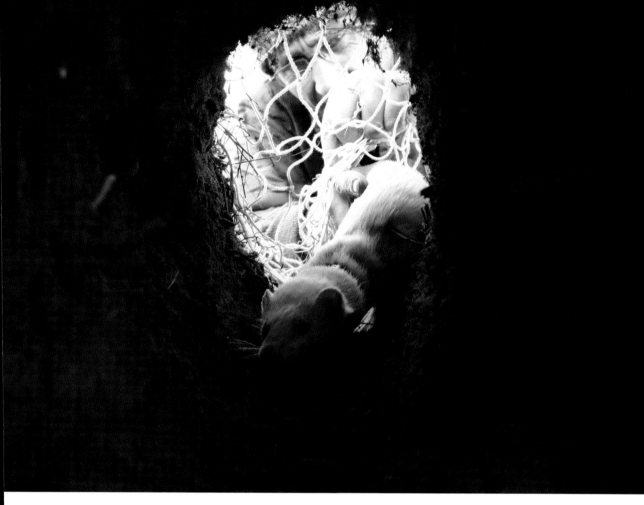

Let the battle commence. (Steven Taylor)

require at least two ferrets, if not three, and of the sort that can take a bit of stick from the rabbit. Just because the warren appears to be small from the surface doesn't necessarily mean that it is small under the ground. The holes may have been backfilled in previous years and the rabbits have had no need to reopen more than one or two. The soil also dictates how much piping is likely to be present, as sand or light soil are easier to move than clay or chalk, so a lot can be shifted in a short space of time, as opposed to chalk, which takes the rabbit many years to shift. The warrens in such an unforgiving substrate as chalk are fraught with danger, as, if the rabbits are reluctant to bolt, retrieving the

ferrets can be extremely difficult due to the impenetrable nature of the ground. Ferrets that don't stick but can kill and move on are the specialists many call upon in such places. Where warrens are situated in soft substrates (sand or light soil), the tunnels can be a lot bigger than the rabbit's body, so the rabbit can move around the warren a lot more freely, often running past a ferret at speed and using this to its advantage. In warrens of hard substrate (heavy clay, chalk or rock), which is harder to excavate, the tunnels are based on the size of the rabbit, therefore it is more difficult for it to outmanoeuvre a ferret in such tight, confined surroundings.

Entering the ferrets can be done in several

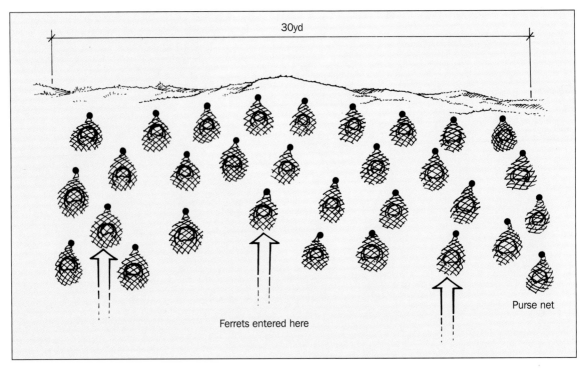

30yd

Purse net

Ferrets entered here

Placing the ferrets evenly over a larger area; in some warrens a lot more ferrets are required than many think.

ways. The most common method is to find a suitable hole that rises as opposed to falls away, then lifting the purse net, entering the ferret and laying the net back down. If only long nets are being used, place the ferret on the ground at the entrance of the warren and allow it to seek out a suitable scent and find its own passage into the warren. What you must never do is force the ferret underground, or push it in and block the hole up with your foot afterwards, as many bad habits are created by this unnecessary action. Let the ferret move about and you will notice by its body language if it is hunting for a scent or just dawdling about aimlessly. Once the ferret is down, you will need to exercise some patience.

For slightly larger warrens, it is advisable to leave the ground to settle for a while so that it can recover from the disturbance caused when setting a lot of nets or cutting back a few branches, unless of course you are just surrounding or placing a couple of long

nets through the hedge or fence line. The ferrets should be entered at regular distances or intervals in order for the team to push the inhabitants into bolting rather than just running about. By using the right amount for that warren, you are forcing an instant decision out of the rabbit. In many warrens I have had great results by working into the wind and placing all the ferrets in at one end. The ferrets then make a blanket-like advance in one direction, forcing the rabbits to move and when they come to the end of the warren they have no option other than to bolt, or pay the consequences.

Work too few ferrets and the rabbits may run around as opposed to bolt; work too many and you may force the rabbits into their stops earlier than you want. By placing the ferrets at the lower entrances of the warren, you are

OPPOSITE: Letting the ferrets work above and below ground. (Steven Taylor)

preventing the rabbits from running deep too early and hopefully forcing them into bolting. In these situations, a slower, more methodical ferret sometimes covers the ground more efficiently than a faster one. In warrens of any size, if the rabbits are running around, I simply add another ferret or two, either to hurry up the bolt or the dig, because if I have to dig to one ferret and a rabbit, I might as well dig to two. Even the smaller warrens sometimes require three or four ferrets to either bolt or force the rabbit into its stop.

On the large warrens you will need extra help to supervise the ferrets, as the last thing you want is to lose sight of any wandering ferrets, especially around game birds or poultry. Place the humans and dogs out of the rabbits' vision, keeping the talking to a minimum and, if possible, using some simple sign language. If you work large warrens by yourself, the extra noise and vibrations of you walking about trying to spot your ferrets or deal with rabbits in the nets can sometimes work against you. The ferrets are again entered at regular intervals, the bottom first for some, the top for others; if you have worked the warren before, you should have built up and retained a map of its internal layout. The number of ferrets required varies with the size and depth of the warren as well as the number of occupants. I have used as many ferrets in a small three-hole warren with many yards of piping as I have in a large warren of shallow depth and not as much piping. Only by experimenting will you see what works for you. Experiencing the different warrens will give you your own opinion of how many ferrets should be used, as each situation is unique.

An important point to note is that, after entering your ferrets, you must remove any active collars fitted to the ferrets in the carrying box/boxes out of receiver range and away from the vicinity that you are working,

OPPOSITE: Patience is needed when working young ferrets to avoid creating any unwanted bad habits. (Steven Taylor)

to avoid false readings if the ferret finder is to be used.

Entering Young and Novice Ferrets

There will come a point when you will be working some new or young ferrets for the first time, especially at the start of the season. The experience these novices gain whilst on their first few trips will release the strong hunting instincts we have bred into them. Young or novice ferrets require patience and understanding when working for the first few outings, usually in conjunction with an experienced ferret. The handling you have given these ferrets from an early age will now be tested to the limit. Place the novice into a warren behind an experienced ferret, stand back and wait for either a rabbit to bolt and hit the net, or the young ferret to run out and get itself tangled up. No matter how often you teach them at home about nets, when working in a real situation the novice will still not be comfortable with purse nets. Patience is required and a calm manner so as not to frighten the ferret and scare it back underground. The same applies to when the ferret surfaces; calmly kneel down and coax the ferret out, even with a bit of rabbit if necessary. Do not lunge at the ferret and scare it back underground, for this will make the ferret skulk at the surface, just out of hands' reach. This bad habit can easily be taught to any ferret, so take the time to retrieve it properly. However much the ferret may be annoying you, you must resist the temptation to lunge at it while it is at the entrance of the hole.

The whole point of ferreting is to bolt the rabbit and many youngsters will take to this very quickly, although some do take a little longer to grasp the situation. Do not become downhearted if in the first few trips the ferrets skip and dance about, however infuriating this may be. Give the slower ferrets a few extra outings in a bid to kick-start their ferreting careers. Unfortunately, you will find out that ferrets are the same as any other animal – some will not work to the standard that you want them to.

WHEN THE FERRET MEETS THE RABBIT

The ferrets are now busy working the warren, using all of their instincts and every ounce of physical presence to seek out the rabbits and persuade them to bolt. The rabbit has two choices to make, bolt or pay the consequences. It may decide to face the ferret head on, try to sit it out in a stop end, or outmanoeuvre

the ferret by continually moving around the different depths of the warren, especially heading straight for the bottom level and sitting tight either in a stop or a larger bowl with other rabbits.

Once the rabbit is aware that the ferret is nearby, it will move on and, in doing so, will make a lot of thumping noise as it travels along the burrows. If you are fortunate, you might get to hear this unforgettable noise. The thumping usually acts as a precursor to a bolt, although it can also mean that the rabbit and ferret are going head to head, or more

Bolt or pay the consequence. (Steven Taylor)

likely head to backside, in a battle for survival. This scenario often makes or breaks a ferret's working pedigree: the ferret will stick to its job and not back down; will force the rabbit to move, staying long enough to get a mark with the ferret finder; or will simply move on. All of these traits have a place in the squad, but if you only have one or two ferrets, time will show you how your ferrets work.

I prefer the ferret to know intimately what a rabbit is, what it means and how it is meant to work one. If the rabbit squares up to the ferret, one small jill may struggle to deliver a killer bite, whereas a well-proportioned hob won't. The ability to kill and move on has its place, the same as a ferret that will stay with a live rabbit but depart from a dead one. Once the ferret has caught up with a rabbit, the noise that can emit through the soil has the ability to turn grown men into children with excitement, raising every hair on the back of your neck, as no matter how many times you hear this noise, each occasion will be different. The rabbit will kick out at the ferret, hiss, spit, bite and claw in a desperate bid for freedom and at times the force of this battle can move the earth on shallower warrens. When the ferret corners the rabbit in a stop end, the outcome will usually be a fight, with a dig or a dispatched rabbit in the nets the result. I have on several occasions bolted rabbits with large bare patches on their rumps, the sign of earlier meetings between rabbit and ferret.

DEALING WITH THE RABBITS IN THE NETS AND AFTERWARDS

Once the rabbit has decided that it has a better chance of survival if it bolts in preference to facing your ferret, and if you have laid your nets correctly and in the right place, you should have the first of many bolted rabbits to deal with. It is worth noting that, contrary to popular belief, not all nets, however skilfully made and laid, will catch every rabbit that bolts into them. The rabbit bolts at all sorts of irregular angles and speeds, and can sometimes nudge a net aside with its head or bolt powerfully enough to pull the peg out of the ground. Once the peg has been released from the ground, the rabbit is able to shake the net off, as the draw cord has no point of friction to purse the net shut.

Once you do have a rabbit in the net, the most important rule is to dispatch it quickly, humanely and efficiently at all times. Dispatch the rabbit while it is still in the net, place the net on the ground straight away, out of the way of the hole and emerging ferret, and quickly reset a new net. This may sound easy, but you would be amazed at just how many struggle with the notion of dispatching a rabbit caught up in a purse net, then resetting a new net.

There are two methods that I favour to dispatch the rabbit in a purse/poke net; a rabbit caught in a long net can and should be dispatched in the same manner.

The first and most practised (dispatch 1) is to hold the rabbit either by the back or shoulder, then place your hand around the neck and stretch whilst slightly tilting the head backwards, ensuring a nice, clean dispatch – what you mustn't do is hold the neck and pull the legs backwards. The amount of force needed to employ this method is minimal, just enough to ensure that the neck has moved a short distance in order to break it; too much force will taint the meat. The young may struggle to dispatch a rabbit this way due to their small hands, but it isn't impossible with careful schooling. It is the technique as opposed to brute strength that does the job. The other method (dispatch 2) is to hold the rabbit in the same manner, but placing your palm under the chin of the rabbit and pushing the chin and neck backwards; another instant clean kill, again technique over brute force.

What I do dislike intensely is the karate chop, an amateurish method of dealing with the rabbit, chopping the rabbit's head with the side of your hand. Often as not, all this method achieves is a bruised hand, severely bruised rabbit meat and an unconscious

Dispatch 1. (Steven Taylor)

Dispatch 2. (Steven Taylor)

Removing a dispatched rabbit from a long net. (Greg Knight)

rather than dead rabbit. If you cannot perform a clean, reliable and humane dispatch with your bare hands, use a 'priest'. This is a hard object that is used to knock the animal on the back of the head to dispatch it. I have been in the presence of some so-called professionals who struggle immensely in dispatching a rabbit. One even resorted to punching the netted rabbit, reminiscent of some bar-room brawl. I often wonder why such a simple task cannot be mastered, because if a person isn't competent to dispatch an animal, should that person be doing it in the first place?

Once the rabbit has been humanely dispatched, you can lay it and the net down,

OPPOSITE: Dispatching a rabbit in the long net. (Steven Taylor)

removing them later when the action has calmed down a bit. A dead rabbit is a lot easier to remove from a net than a live one. If the rabbit is still alive, by removing it from the net you will be giving it a possible avenue of escape if it happens to kick, scratch or bite you and you are shocked into releasing your grip. Once dispatched, the nerves of the rabbit may remain active, giving the impression that it is still alive. On many occasions with the awful chopping method, many rabbits have simply been knocked unconscious and have awoken several minutes later to run off. If you are working with such a ferreter, always lay the rabbits inside a long net if possible, rather than on the outside, just in case.

When resetting the nets, a new net is laid to replace the original net just after the rabbit

Once the action has ceased, deal with the rabbits. (Steven Taylor)

OPPOSITE: *Swift re-netting to prevent an unnecessary escapee. (Steven Taylor)*

has been dispatched from the original net. Often the ferreter will block the empty hole for a few seconds with his foot to prevent a second rabbit from escaping until a new net can be laid. Always carry a few spare nets around with you whilst ferreting.

Once the rabbit has been dispatched and has cooled, the first thing to do is to 'pee' the rabbit, that is, empty the bladder of its urine, otherwise this will taint the meat if left inside the body. Place the rabbit on its back in one hand and with the other run your thumb down its stomach and the urine will flow out. This doesn't always happen as the rabbit might be empty, or might have emptied itself in the process of the bolt, capture or dispatch.

WHAT IF THE RABBITS AREN'T BOLTING?

The time when the rabbits aren't bolting is when both the ferret and ferreter will be truly tested. In times of little action you must decide whether to wait it out, or change your plan of action to outwit the rabbit into bolting. The ferret, as described above, will try its hardest with its powerful claws to persuade the rabbit to bolt, but once the rabbit is in the stop end, the ferret is unable to bolt it or get behind to kill it, so the locator will be called for. If the rabbits are on the move, you must either wait or place another ferret or two in, which is my preferred option. The more time spent ferreting, the more you notice certain oddities, for example why the rabbits may be refusing to bolt when conditions seem near perfect. The presence of young rabbits can cause problems, as these have little tendency to bolt and just run around underground until the ferret catches them. Being small, nippy and agile, these youngsters ensure that the ferret wastes a lot of time and energy trying to curtail their activity. A few good strong jills that will kill and move on will prove their worth in such a situation.

Always remember to extract the urine in order to avoid tainting the meat. (Steven Taylor)

If they don't want to bolt, they won't. (Steven Taylor)

Nobody can experience what goes on underground between the rabbit and the ferret, but with a few years of digging them both out and seeing the results of many a heated encounter, I have a pretty good idea why the rabbits just didn't fancy fleeing from home. The fact that the rabbit could have been educated by a previous ferreting trip, or because instinct kicks in, may mean it knows what is coming, as it has managed to survive a few previous encounters simply by running about and hiding in a stop end and sitting it out. This isn't going to do any good if a good ferret finder is used, although only if the ferret stays with the rabbit long enough for me to get a mark. It is amazing that many rabbits get used to the sounds of cars, quad bikes or livestock, but flee at the crack of a dried twig or when they catch the scent of a net being laid, as many rabbits over the course of the year will bolt if they hear nets being laid, before a ferret has even been entered. If the area is host to stoats and weasels hunting regularly, this will also teach the rabbit about survival. In certain situations, the instinct to survive seems to be getting stronger, possibly passed on in the genes of surviving parents. In areas of no interference, the rabbit is usually reluctant to budge, whereas in other interfered-with areas they will bolt freely. Another reason could be that the rabbits have just fed so are not as alert to bolt. The faintest hint of trouble and these rabbits seek out the stops or go to the deep chambers and pipes at the bottom of the warren. Another major factor from the turn of the new year is that if a rabbit is pregnant it will not bolt as readily as a rabbit that has just given birth or is not pregnant at all.

Are Some Rabbits Easier to Bolt Than Others?

It is only when you look at the geology, topography and history of the United Kingdom, the areas hunted and how often, that you obtain a realistic picture of what Britain is like to ferret. Historically, many areas have had and always will hold large populations of rabbits. On many locations, you look at the habitat and come to the conclusion that the rabbits would struggle to survive there, but they don't. Likewise, land that appears to be ideally suited may have very few resident rabbits. A lot depends on how often the land is hunted – the rifle, snare, net, trap, ferret and dog can do serious damage to a local population if done competently. If rabbits are continually harassed and controlled, they will be stripped of their ability to repopulate, but if the land is left alone for a period if time, the remaining reservoirs of rabbits will readily fill any void. We have already drawn the conclusion that every area of the UK contains a population of rabbits, some in greater numbers than others, but we must be honest with ourselves over the difficulty or ease with which many of these rabbits are annually caught. This is a controversial subject that divides the opinions of the nation's ferreters, but wherever in the UK you ferret, it is human nature to believe instinctively that your rabbits aren't the easiest in the world to catch; only a fool would admit that they just ferret easy rabbits. What confuses the situation even more is that nobody has come up with a credible explanation as to why some rabbits do indeed appear easier to catch than others.

When we talk about easy rabbits, what do we really mean? Easy is as easy does, but please don't jump to the same conclusion as many ferreters when using such an emotive word. The definition of easy is something that is free from trouble or anxiety, is relaxed or pleasant and compliant. Is a rabbit that has taken a lot of hard work from the ferrets to persuade it to bolt, or a deep, troublesome dig, easier than a rabbit that has eagerly bolted at the first sniff of danger? Rabbits caught in such a way generally live in areas of little disturbance by man, sometimes in shallower warrens where digging is quick and relatively easy. Populations of such high density ensure a passage to ferret freely with fewer hold-ups and, when a snag is encountered, the next warren within a few metres is usually

OPPOSITE: Easy is as easy does. (Steven Taylor)

occupied, although all rabbits that live on your permission still need to be found and bolted.

In the majority of the UK, the encroachment of the urban population has divided up the countryside into segments with roads, towns and rail links, although in some areas there are still large tracts of unpopulated land, for example land that is not put down for crops but managed (or unmanaged) heath or moorland. Rabbits on land such as this will most likely not have experienced what humans and dogs can mean to their survival. Any land with more rabbits per acre and less disturbance by humans should bear more fruitful excursions than land disturbed more often and holding fewer rabbits. A lot of ferreters, especially with dogs, like to ferret such open warrens and will travel great distances to experience the sheer volume of rabbits at their disposal. Such confidence-boosters, especially for young and inexperienced dogs, are usually in spots that haven't been touched and are left for such outings. However, such areas are now becoming scarcer.

For those wanting to film or take pictures, these areas present a greater degree of success, with many more chances to get the right footage without the obstructions of dense undergrowth that can take away the main focus of the picture. You will always get results ferreting such spots, but in other areas, just because the land on top appears open, it doesn't necessarily mean that underneath it is shallow, as in the majority of cases it won't be. The warrens I know at home or around the country may be nice and open to look at, but they are also very deep. The film or photograph doesn't show the full extent of the subject matter, that is, the three-dimensional aspect of a warren.

Another of the must-have pieces of equipment, the cameraman. (Greg Knight)

Rabbits in deep warrens have to be pushed very hard into bolting; digging isn't always an option, especially in chalk or sandy warrens of considerable depth. This is where a ferret that can kill and move on is a valuable asset. I am no different to the rest when it comes to underestimating the depth of a warren, but it is an experience gained and one you must learn from quickly. Rabbits in deep warrens feel safer in the depths, sitting it out rather than freely bolting and running the gauntlet. In my area, the eager bolters are generally those in hedgerows or thick cover, where the security of the foliage offers a smokescreen. Having this safety blanket enables them either to bolt at full speed or sneak out, although these cunning coneys are no match for a cleverly placed net.

Competent ferreters will catch rabbits anywhere, but especially on land they know and understand intimately. Their equipment and animals are designed for such terrain. But I have also been ferreting in locations I thought would be easy, only to come unstuck, whereas some places I have dreaded ferreting, the rabbits obliged without the slightest hesitation. It just goes to show how nature can be unpredictable at times. At the end of the day, the size of the bag can be misleading and give a false impression of the day's ferreting. It is only when the day is put into context with the rabbit population in the ferreted area that you see a realistic picture. A ferreter who is catching fewer rabbits may be doing a better job than one who is catching far more rabbits but on land holding a lot more.

The easiest rabbit is always the one that has already been caught and dispatched. (Greg Knight)

By calculating the rabbit population on your permission, divided by the amount caught, this should equal the percentage controlled. In an area where the rabbit population is small and therefore fewer rabbits are caught, the percentage controlled may be higher than if you are on land with a large population of rabbits, even if you catch a lot more rabbits. The areas with a smaller population often dictate the urgency and importance of catching every possible rabbit, as a single rabbit on barren land is worth twenty on laden land.

When controlling rabbits in gardens and paddocks it is important to get every last rabbit. The majority of gardens and paddocks may only have a few rabbits, either under a shed or a stable, but you do not want to leave a single rabbit behind when you leave, because it is certain to sit directly in front of the farmer or occupant as soon as you have left. Such escapees often guarantee a quick revisit, but may endanger the bill being paid. This is where experience teaches you that once a warren has been ferreted, no matter the size of it, you should build up and retain an instant mental map of the construction in your mind ready for the next time. Knowing where the rabbits run, where the stop ends are located, how much piping is underground and how deep it goes is all information you must store inside your mind if you are to progress and make your next visit just as, if not more, successful.

LOCATING YOUR FERRETS

The way to tell how proficient some are at ferreting isn't the number of rabbits caught, but how they deal with the situations when things go wrong. For example, when the ferret is sticking with a rabbit or is trapped between two dead rabbits, you will need to find it in order to dig it out. In Chapter 5 on ferret retrieval devices, I outline how to find

OPPOSITE: *The ferret finder being used.* *(Steven Taylor)*

the ferret, place a marker where it is and either wait or dig.

Sometimes you cannot find the ferret, as the warren may be deeper than you had anticipated, the ferret might have sneaked out unseen, or your finder is on the blink. If you are fully aware of what is going on, you can be confident that the ferret won't have sneaked out to do some freelance hunting elsewhere, plus you checked your equipment before you set out for the day, so the ferret must be down deep. Fortunately, we now have a new design of ferret finder which lets you know how deep the ferret is and where. With the Mk3, you can stand away from most warrens and find the location of the ferrets without moving too much, thus preventing disturbance to the proceedings underground. Once you have located the ferret, the time is right to lose a few pounds and start digging.

The Dig

Life generally holds few guarantees apart from death, but, for a ferreter, digging is also a given. Ferreting can and will offer problems from time to time; many are avoidable, but sooner or later you will have to test your digging skills, like it or not. Digging is how you will be required to get your ferret back above ground in order for you to crack on and not waste countless hours waiting for it to return to the surface when you know full well it is stuck on a rabbit in a stop end.

The terrain must be taken into consideration when digging, as well as the tools needed and the amount of time the dig will take. The condition and type of ground is also important, not forgetting the hidden dangers such as glass, metal or baling twine. The spade or spades you decide to use should be ones that are best suited to the ground you are about to work and not a spade that is in vogue or convenient to carry.

We must not forget the role of the probe either (*see* Chapter 4); I am amazed at just how many ferreters do not employ this piece of equipment. Digging without such an essential piece of equipment not only adds time

The hunter and the hunted. (Author)

to your excavation, but restricts you from en-suring that you have safely broken through to the pipe. With the soil condition affecting the ferret finder's strength of signal and the rab-bits' ability to channel their tunnels on top of each other as well as side by side or vertically together, you could break through to an empty tunnel, while the actual position of the ferret could be just inches behind that empty cham-ber. A word of caution is required when using the probe, though, as you spike the ground and everything that lies beneath the spike's end. You must use a probe with a rounded but blunt point to avoid injury to your ferrets, but it can and does spook the rabbit into making that one final push for freedom as the ferret backs off when the ground starts to open just as you break through. It is the same as the final spit of soil; many times the rabbit has tried to escape not through the tunnel system but up the spade as it has broken through to the piping.

OPPOSITE: *To dig or not to dig, that is the question. (Steven Taylor)*

To avoid a false impression, clean the fur off the ferret's claws. (Steven Taylor)

The dig starts with the ferreter deciding to find his ferrets using his ferret finder (for further information about ferret finders, *see* Chapter 5). It finds the centre of the sweet spot and the actual depth of the ferret. All you have to do now is dig down and get them both out.

The ferret has either got a single rabbit or as many as three, four or more bottled up in a stop end, has stopped a rabbit mid-pipe, or has killed one or more rabbits and has become trapped. The ferret will have to be dug out, or move the dead rabbit, or it will need to eat its way past the body blocking the escape route. The rabbit warren was built by the rabbit for the rabbit and is a deadly place for the much smaller animals that frequent such places. The smaller, thinner slimline ferret will have difficulty scaling some of these tunnels, especially the longer, deeper vertical shafts that we encounter in warrens that are on flattish land.

Once the spot has been located, if it is turf, crops or plants, you should carefully take off a clean slab from the surface which will be replaced after the hole has been filled in. If the land is bare earth, this is not as essential as there is nothing to make good. After every dig it is advisable to ensure that you leave the land as you found it. With the use of the shoulder, foot and hands, a hole is then dug using your spade. Any root protruding and hampering the dig can be removed with the use of secateurs or your spade's sharp edge. The hole is then dug, cleaning each side to ensure minimal soil spillage and seepage into the bottom of the hole. Obviously a deep hole will require a bigger starting area to work down without worrying about the sides caving in.

Once you are a good 6–12in (15–30cm) from the signal's peak, use the probe to probe the soil to find the exact position of the void that is the pipe, if the probe will go into the ground that far. One of the facts that many overlook when using the ferret finder and complaining that its depth is out, is the way in which a warren's pipe is constructed. It could be up to 8in (20cm) high in certain sandy spots local to me, so you might only be a few inches from the pipe, but the reading implies a good deal more because the area where the ferret is wearing the collar is close to the ground.

An injury to your ferret is highly likely if you continue to dig haphazardly without stopping to check for depth and movement. Once the probe has located the pipe, you have the choice of using your hands, trowel or spade to break through carefully to the pipe holding the ferret and rabbit(s).

In an ideal world you would never experience obstacles such as stone, flint, roots, metal, cables, rubbish or concrete, but unfortunately we do, with the worst being baling twine. I carry a small breaker's demolition bar that I use on many occasions to break through or at least crack open hard substances. It may be noisy, but it is very effective and the chances are by the time you have dug down, the noise and vibrations would have alerted the resident rabbits anyway, so a little more noise will do no harm.

A seasoned ferret will move away from the rabbit, unless trapped, just as you are about to break through, but extra care is a must when digging in sand. Sand can pour as in an egg timer and can be lethal for your ferret as no natural air bubble is formed, unlike in other soil substances. Once you have broken through, it will still be dark in the pipe, so to see what is really going on, I find a small torch always comes in handy. A word of warning though when breaking through the pipes. Once the ferret has been removed, just err on the side of caution when reaching in to pull something out as the ferret may have encountered rats, stoats, weasels or hedgehogs, especially if they are cornered.

Sometimes, though, a ferret will be able to move the rabbit away from the spot to which you are digging, or the rabbit isn't dead and has moved away with the ferret in pursuit. When this occurs, snap a little branch or stick and feel around the pipe where you think the rabbit may be. When the stick is removed, usually a small amount of the rabbit's fur

Sitting it out. (Author)

will have stuck to the end to signify its presence. This is a handy way to find a rabbit if the soil has collapsed, or you are digging in sand or sandy soil, which has a tendency to cave in due to the structure of the substrate. At times you can draw these rabbits out with a bramble, but remember to cut off some of its thorns on the end you are going to handle so you don't cut yourself too badly, but, to be honest, these occasions are very rare as usually the ferret is still with the rabbit in a stop end. If you work a lot of ferrets, you are likely to find that multiple rabbits will be trapped mid-pipe with a ferret to the front and rear. This is why a lot of rabbits in bigger warrens are dug to mid-pipe.

When the ferret has been removed, it is best to box it up or get a friend to hold it out of harm's way (if you remove the ferret it pays to clean the claws of fur so as to avoid future confusion about whether or not it has been on

a fresh rabbit). If the rabbit feels loose in its stop, there is a good chance that it is not on its own and more rabbits are behind the one you have just dug to and pulled out. The most I have pulled out was five, but on many occasions I have pulled two or three out after a dig. When feeling about in the blind in a dark tunnel, be vigilant against the dangers of trapped animals, flint, glass and metallic objects, all of which could cause injury.

When the rabbit is stuck hard, you may find it difficult to remove as it will have puffed up its body to form a vacuum between itself and the surrounding walls. The legs are tucked under and the tail is firmly against the ground. Many think the rabbit's tail should be showing, but a stuck rabbit presents nothing to the ferret other than a wall of fur. It is then harder for the ferret to find a piece of the rabbit to grip and pull at. Usually you would grab a back leg and pull, or if mid-pipe it might be the ears or head. If you cannot do this, you must think like a rabbit. What does the rabbit do when confronted by the ferret? It kicks out. By mimicking the ferret and either poking or prodding the rabbit's rear quarters, it is then duty bound to kick out to defend itself. Once the rabbit has kicked out, the seal has been broken and you have the chance to grab a leg. Many cuts and bruises are gained but so are rabbits. All rabbits, however caught, must be dispatched as quickly and humanely as possible.

After each rabbit has been removed from your dig, always check the piping, or stop to see if there are any more rabbits in there. Sometimes during a dig, the ferret will move around due to the noise and vibrations, or there may be another rabbit in a stop, or your

ferret just may not be interested in staying put with a bottled-up rabbit. When multiple ferrets are used, sometimes their transmitters may confuse the receiver, so a bit of previous practice is invaluable, as the receiver will always pick up the strongest signal. If the rabbit is mid-pipe, be careful whilst digging, especially in soft soil or sand, as the spoil (loose soil) may bury both rabbit and ferrets. If the ferret consistently moves and it goes to the same area, place a visible marker and dig at a later time. Several rabbits are usually located this way.

All excavations must be back-filled and a little extra earth added to compensate for the void you have just dug, especially if a turf/crop slab has been removed. I am amazed at how many people scratch their heads after filling

Out you come. (Author)

in a hole, to find that it is 6in (15cm) short of soil. The tunnel you have just dug to is a void and you have broken its supported roof, so the earth filling the tunnel has to come from the soil you have just dug through.

A lot of ferreters fight shy of digging because they do not want to spoil the warren's workings for a later date, but my experience of the rabbit is that if it wants to go back, it will. This is one of the aspects that separate sport from control. Yes, new stop ends are formed from the spoils of earth when a hole has been filled in. Often the rabbits will dig this little area out again, but on the positive side you now have first-hand experience of where they are and can second-guess where the ferret is likely to end up when you ferret that warren next time.

AT THE END OF THE DAY

The secret to good ferreting is knowing when to stop, having the knack of saying to others that it is time to pick up the ferrets and either move on or ship out. Too much time can be wasted waiting for stubborn rabbits to bolt, so you must either dig them out or leave them for another time, it is your call.

It is a mistake to fall into the trap of thinking 'Let's just do one more warren'. Nothing is guaranteed to tempt fate more than a ferreter eager for that last rabbit to make the day complete. At the end of a hectic day, the light will be failing, the animals physically and mentally tired and the rabbits wary; now is the time for things not to go to plan. In the depths of winter, the light will be failing at 3.30 in the afternoon, but come March it is an hour later, so the time of year and weather conditions will have a large bearing on this particular decision. Too many times have I heard tales of ferrets being put to ground in unsuitable warrens as the light is fading fast. Cut your losses and get out while the going is good. At the end of the day, the decision is yours, but make that decision wisely.

OPPOSITE: Quit while you are ahead.
(Steven Taylor)

Retrieving the Ferrets
Once you have decided to call it a day, or the ferrets have finished their work and seem uninterested in the warren, simply pick them up and put them in their carrying boxes. Some youngsters may need a bit of persuasion by tempting them out with a piece of rabbit, but as a rule, if they are used to being handled and ferreted, pick them up and replace them in their warm, dry and secure transport boxes.

Picking Up the Nets
Only once all of the ferrets have been accounted for should you start to pick up the nets. You risk losing rabbits by picking them up too early and after you have waited for your ferret to come out, if it finds a fresh scent you may have to sit back down again. There are ways of counting nets, for example by having elastic bands on each net and placing these on your wrist, by carrying them about in tens in separate bags within a bag, or by the good old tried and tested method of remembering where you put them. After all the nets have been picked up, go back for another check just in case one has slipped your vigilant search, especially if two or three people have been laying nets that the other doesn't know about. It also pays to check your pockets, as it is easy to put nets in and forget about them.

Backfilling the Holes
In certain situations, you will be required to backfill the holes after you have ferreted the warren. This serves several purposes. In the first instance, it will provide a barrier against the rabbits just walking back into an open and spare warren. If you backfill each warren after ferreting them, when you ferret the next warren, if any rabbits escape and head back to these previously ferreted holes, they will find them blocked and a dog or gun can mop these up as they struggle to dig back underground. However, the main reason for filling in is to get a chance to see if the rabbits have moved in or out.

Once the holes have been backfilled and not just caved in, the way to tell if the rabbit

has resurfaced is to study how the hole has been opened up. If it has been opened up as a neat hole, probably the size of a cricket ball, then the rabbit has surfaced from inside, as the spoil has gone inwards. If the rabbit has dug in, the spoil will be on the outside of the hole as it normally is. Although the vast majority of ferreters take these sorts of signs for granted, if no one is ever told, how are you to know any different? If you want to know how a hole is being used before you have time to ferret it, place a stem from a weed or a light twig over the centre of the hole and, depending on its movement, you will instantly know if anything has gone in or out. If the twig fell outwards, the rabbit has emerged; inwards and it has gone into the warren, pushing the obstruction down. Make sure that whatever

you use, it isn't too big to deter the rabbit from entering.

During the day, instead of piling all of the rabbits on to of each other, pee, leg and hang up the rabbits by their back legs, or place your game carrier in a suitable place like a tree or hedge, for the rabbits to air. This ensures that when you come to gut and skin the rabbits the meat will be in tip-top condition. If you sell the catch, the presentation of unmarked and uncrushed rabbits will be welcomed, earning you a better price for the goods. Once the ferrets and nets have been collected, all that is needed is to take care of the catch. Dig a large-enough hole and proceed to gut the rabbits, filling the hole slowly with the innards of the catch. Once finished, fill the hole in and put the rabbits in the vehicle.

By removing the rabbit guts in the field, you preserve the quality of the meat and prevent it from being contaminated. (Steven Taylor)

OPPOSITE: Count them in and out. (Steven Taylor)

171

Make the hole big enough to backfill sufficiently. (Steven Taylor)

Taking off the Collars and Boxing Up

Once the ferrets have been picked up for the journey home, a drink of water and a quick check over will be in order to determine whether any injuries have been sustained during their day's outing. It is commonplace also to check them for ticks, because although few rabbits have been caught with ticks attached to them, their warrens and especially any bedding are legendary habitats for such creatures. Once every ferret has been collected, their collars can be removed, the batteries taken out and placed in a safe container ready for the next outing. The ferrets and their carrying boxes are then placed inside the vehicles ready for the journey home.

AILMENTS AND WORK-RELATED INJURIES

Whilst working, all animals, including us, will pick up an injury or two and in extreme cases fatalities are reported. When looking over the ferret for injuries, you must pay particular attention to the head and feet. In a course of a winter's ferreting, the ferrets will pick up countless ticks from the warrens and will get kicked, scratched and bitten, not only by the rabbit but whatever else is underground, be it a snake, rat or stoat, to name but a few. Careful consideration must be given to the rat and fox, as both of these will live side by side with the rabbit. Where rats are present, leptospirosis (Weil's disease) will

The result of one too many bunny punches. (Author)

be a potential danger if you have any cuts or abrasions on your body.

Fleas

The ferrets, via the rabbits, can pick these up underground or in the hutch at feeding time. I have found that ferrets do not appear to pick up fleas constantly, unlike ticks.

Ticks

Ticks are one of the most underestimated but potentially dangerous creatures in the UK. The ferret sometimes picks them up whilst working, but mainly whilst being fed on rabbit with its jacket (fur) still on, or through straw used for bedding. They normally get picked up in the feet, ears or around the head/neck area. The tick lies dormant and then jumps onto the host animal. Once fed they appear bloated and, unless treated, will then drop off and complete its life cycle.

To remove a tick you can use a tick removal tool but I favour using an authorized flea and tick spray that I get from my vets to use on my dogs. This kills the tick and prevents infection from parts of the tick left in the ferret, which would be the case if force was used in its removal. Do not freeze or burn the tick, or smother it with petroleum jelly or any other liquid solution that isn't authorized for this use, as this will stimulate it to regurgitate its stomach contents, increasing the chance of infection. For more information see www.bada-uk.org.

Hitching a lift. (Author)

Snakes

One creature that we are coming into contact with more is the snake. Although there is only one indigenous poisonous snake, the adder (*Vipera berus*), other species of snakes may have escaped from private collections. Snake bites are uncommon in the UK and, if a bite occurs, it is usually from a non-venomous snake, but unless you can identify the snake, it is advisable to administer first aid and seek medical help as soon as possible, on the assumption that the snake may have been venomous. I have encountered snakes on a few occasions, but only know of two or three cases where ferrets or dogs have been bitten, fatally in the ferret's case. On land renowned for having snakes and especially if you are ferreting in the summer or late autumn, just be aware of the dangers. The majority of bites will occur in the summer months in areas of long grass or heath. Fatalities are rare and the last recorded human fatality in the UK was thirty years ago. Following an adder bite, pain will immediately be felt at the bite site and local swelling will occur. If no swelling has occurred at the bite site within two hours it is unlikely that the snake's venom has entered the body.

If a person or animal has, or may have, been bitten, treatment prior to transfer to hospital/veterinary hospital should consist only of reassurance to the patient and immobilization of the limb. A bandage should not be applied in this instance as over-tightening of the bandage may lead to complications.

Rats

Obviously while out ferreting and especially when digging, from time to time you will get cuts or abrasions to your skin; the same applies to the ferrets and dogs. The rat population is on the increase due to changes in our living habits. In the countryside, the numbers are growing because of the increase of cover crops and bird feeders on shoots. These attract rats, as they are an easy source of food, so rats are now resident in or around the warren and ferreters run the risk of catching leptospirosis (Weil's disease).

This is a disease that affects both humans and animals. The bacteria have a wide range of symptoms and if left unchecked could be severely damaging and in some cases fatal. The symptoms range from pale yellowish skin, vomiting, nausea, diarrhoea and a rash. To survive, the bacteria must have a wet environment in which to pass on to their victim, usually by direct contact with contaminated water, damp soil or indeed the rats themselves. The disease enters the body through cuts and abrasions. Whilst ferreting we are always digging in soil, retrieving ferrets, but, more importantly, rabbits. The rabbit can inadvertently spread this disease by its sharp claws that are always in contact with the ground. Scratches do occur to the ferreter from the rabbit's claws, so the risk of infection is always present. It is prudent to have a method of cleaning your hands and have a first-aid kit handy just in case a plaster or bandage is required.

Foxes

Obviously, if we are placing an animal underground to bolt another animal, it may not always be a rabbit that comes out. Over the years I have been present when a number of animals have vacated the warrens, from little owls, partridges and cats, but the most dangerous to the ferrets is the fox. The fox is an opportunist and at a certain time of the year, it will look for somewhere safe to give birth or just to shelter and have a snooze. If disturbed by a ferret whilst sleeping, the fox usually bolts freely as it has been surprised and its instinct is to flee. However, when the fox is fully aware of its surroundings or has a litter to protect, it will stay and fight, with the result that the ferret may be injured or killed.

The result of a foxy encounter. (Greg Knight)

Always do your utmost to ensure that all of your ferrets have a safe return home.

WHAT TO DO IF A FERRET IS MISSING OR TRAPPED

Sometimes, though, you may have to make that journey home a ferret light, as one may be missing in action. I have spoken to those who have lost ferrets, but to this day I have not lost one myself, although I have had many long waits and some deep digs. As a result, I tend to keep the smaller warrens for the latter parts of the day as they are normally easier to dig in a relatively short space of time. The usual reasons behind the loss of a ferret are that the ferreter wasn't using a ferret finder; it was faulty, most likely with flat batteries on the collar; or the ferreter was working large warrens late on. While we all experience these sorts of problems from time to time, we owe it to our ferrets to try to ensure that we have a fail-safe way of getting them back when things don't go according to plan. In Chapter 5, I have explained about the various methods of retrieval using the ferret finder and in 99 per cent of situations this works well. I have also outlined in this chapter the several other less orthodox methods of ferret retrieval that you can try. However, ultimately, if the ferret does not want to leave a rabbit, it won't and it is essentially only doing what we want it to. If it is trapped by a dead rabbit, at least it will have food and moisture in order to survive until it can shift the corpse either by eating a gap or by pulling it aside and in this case it may take a day or two for the ferret to surface.

If the ferret still hasn't surfaced and you are losing daylight and having to think about the journey home, secure the ferret if it resurfaces in the trap box, a spare carrying box or a drop pit. In Chapter 5 the trap box and open ferret-carrying box are explained in greater detail, but not many ferreters carry a spare carrying box and if more than one ferret is used, how are the remaining ferrets going to travel back? For this scenario a hole can be dug and a branch placed over the top of the hole with a piece of rabbit meat attached to it via a piece of string (or the draw cord from a net). The idea is for the ferret, once on the surface, to try to reach the food and fall into the pit until the owner can retrieve their lost ferret. Unfortunately the ferret isn't the largest or only predator about at night, and can become prey itself. The trap box is the best option as the ferret will be safe and secure overnight. Sometimes it can take a few days for the ferret to eat through or move a rabbit, or negotiate a difficult climb. The majority of losses occur on ferrets without a serviceable ferret finder collar fitted, especially the old 8ft models. I advocate and use the improved Mk 3 ferret finder as it has a range of 16ft, so although I probably have no intention of digging 16ft, at least I know where the ferrets are. Looking

at the warren sensibly, very few ferreters ferret warrens deeper than 20ft or so.

FINISHING OFF AT HOME

Once the car has pulled up, the doors swing open and you wearily droop out of the car, the first priority is to get the dogs out, closely followed by the ferrets and to put them away. Check them over for any injuries before placing them back home with a nice meal and warm bedding for them to dream about the next outing. No matter how tired you feel or how much your hands and perhaps face are tingling with the venom of those small stinging nettles that have placed a temporary curse on your skin, you have a job or two to do before you can soak away the day in a nice warm bath.

The stiff or hot drink will have to wait; all the team have been working hard today. Once the animals have been fed, watered and bedded down, it is time to get the catch out of the car or van. Hang, box or prepare the rabbits for the freezer, as rabbits that have been left in the car look shoddy and unprofessional when presenting them to those who are paying good money for this excellent meat. The gear I use is left in the van all the time, but I make sure the collars are removed and batteries taken out as we finish; the nets are neatly folded up in several bags, but if they have been out in foul weather I sometimes air them a bit in the ferret shed. I use my nets on a daily basis, so they are never allowed to fester away in a game bag for weeks on end, which is certainly something to avoid if you ferret only occasionally.

If you are using the hemp nets, extra care must be taken to ensure that these last for years, which they will if cared for properly. The jobs that have to be done when you get home may seem a bind at times, but as these little actions ensure your kit lasts for a very long time, in the long run they are worth that little bit of inconvenience.

CHAPTER SEVEN

Why We
Do It

When you step back and take a long, hard look at ferreting, it can be an unsociable activity, practised in all weathers, silently, usually alone or sometimes with a friend, but it fulfils our inner instinct of the hunter-gatherer. At the end of each ferreting trip, we usually have some tales to tell, aches and pains to recover from, but, above all, we have some rabbits to take home. Whatever way you choose to catch the rabbit, ferreting as pest control has the advantage over the more toxic methods of control, in that the rabbits will be suitable as a food source. This will mean some extra income at the end of a day's ferreting; it can be a nice little earner when you have a ready market for all your clean ferreted rabbits, caught on the land's largest free-range farm, our countryside. It should be noted that wild rabbit cannot be labelled as organic because we cannot guarantee that the land on which it has been eating is organic land, registered with the organic societies.

In the UK, the majority of our wild rabbits are exported. In the United Kingdom only around 2–3,000 tonnes per annum are produced, the majority farmed, and a further 5,000 tonnes are imported from China, Hungary and Poland. The reluctance to eat wild rabbit meat is still evident in the United Kingdom since the initial outbreak of myxomatosis over fifty years ago. This reluctance goes against today's logic, as people are still eating cattle after BSE and blue tongue, lamb and pork after foot and mouth and poultry after bird flu. Ironically, in France where the myxomatosis outbreak originated, the rabbit is utilized nationally as a food source with an average annual consumption of 9lb (4kg) per head of the population.

Up until the 1950s, when myxomatosis changed how our nation perceived eating rabbit meat, it was a valuable commodity and regular trains were laid on to transport thousands of rabbit carcasses from all over the UK to markets such as Smithfield in London. As we progress into the twenty-first century, we are always looking for healthier options, rather than the cheap, mass-produced convenience food that is turning our nation's population into obese couch potatoes. Convenience food has replaced the traditional family meal, as fewer families are sitting down together at the table to eat home-cooked meals. Such meals provided an excellent opportunity for conversation and for children to be taught manners and social skills. Eating alone usually results in a meal that is of less nutritional value than the traditional meal eaten as a group.

With the rise in the popularity of and reliance upon convenience foods, it is no surprise that the nation's health is suffering, along with its ability to cook appropriate, nutritious food, especially off the bone. Falling into the trap of conveniently going down to the supermarket on an evening after work is turning the nation lazy. Not just content with purchasing meat produced from farms with lower welfare standards, this mass-produced food is lower in price due to foreign imports, another setback for the nation's struggling farmers.

The majority of the UK's wild rabbit meat is exported. (Steven Taylor)

Because of this downward trend in healthy eating, the media is trying to educate the nation about what is a healthier diet. Rabbit meat is growing in popularity in the same vein as most game, especially as the popular press and the television celebrity chefs are leaning towards using such an environmentally friendly, free-range product. Even the staunchest of opponents to country pursuits find it hard to present a sensible argument against the fundamentals of ferreting. I can justify what I do by providing an environmentally friendly, non-toxic method of legitimate pest control and by using the rabbits caught as food for both human and animal consumption; nothing is wasted.

OPPOSITE: The hunter-gatherer. (Steven Taylor)

From Michelin-rated restaurants to the small country cottage in complete solitude, the rabbit is once more being reintroduced to the dining table. Cost and convenience will always be the major factor in household shopping budgets, but when it comes to nutritional value, wild rabbit ticks all the right boxes. Wild rabbit is not only kept in a free-range environment, but it is leaner, tastier (with a subtle gamey flavour) and more natural than farmed rabbit. With a low fat content and a high protein count, along with being a good source of iron, phosphorus, vitamin B12 and niacin, the rabbit is a healthy alternative to the customary poultry, pork, beef or lamb.

Nothing from the rabbit carcass is wasted, with the prime cuts being used for human consumption and the leftovers fed to the dogs,

hawks or ferrets. The growing popularity in feeding BARF (Bone And Raw Food) to our dogs is ensuring that even rifled or shot-gunned rabbits have a use. The stories of burying or discarding the day's catch on the way home fill me with horror. How are we supposed to look our opponents in the eye and defend what we do if we blatantly waste good food in this way?

The respect we show the rabbit starts with the dispatch. It must be clean, precise, effective and, above all, humane. Any undue stress on the animal will only affect its meat. Once the rabbit has cooled, expel the urine from the body (*see* Chapter 6) to ensure that it doesn't taint the meat. The rabbits should then be hung up by their back legs to cool and air in a tree or bush. The rabbits should not be left in a pile on top of each other as this will result in a poor quality carcass. To receive the premium rate they must be in prime condition, something which in the early weeks of the season needs a lot of thought. With the onset of warmer and wetter winters, flies are often rampant well into the winter and rabbits can easily get flyblown before they can get back to the vehicle. The regular or potential customer can be put off by this fact. To counteract this many are placing the caught rabbits inside a simple fly-proof bag until they can offload the carcasses to the seller, or gut and skin them ready for use.

The rabbit is best gutted and skinned while it is still warm as the skin separates easier and the guts will not have the time to bloat or break, thus contaminating the meat. The rabbit is therefore prepared almost straight away, unlike hares, which are usually hung for a while to strengthen the flavour of the meat.

As of 1 January 2006, new legislation has been introduced. If the carcasses are to be sold on, there are new rules which must be observed by individuals who supply game and venison (sale or gift). The rules are required to meet a European directive on food safety and are being supervised by the Food Standards Agency (FSA). Organizations such as BASC (British Association for Shooting and Conservation) run courses on this subject in order to ensure that whatever quarries you are after, you stay within the law. The requirement for training comes from an EC regulation (853/2004), which aims to improve food hygiene standards across the European Union.

Gutting and skinning a rabbit is fairly straightforward, but you must first remember to expel the urine from the rabbit if this has not already been done. Once the rabbit is dry, paunch or gut it. To do this, carefully insert the tip of a very sharp knife under the fur and stomach skin and slide from the rear of the abdomen to between the front legs. Many put their hands in and pull out the contents, but I place a knife under and flick the contents out, thus avoiding the mess on your hands just in case you have no means of washing them afterwards. If you don't want the rabbit's lingering scent on your hands, disposable latex gloves are readily available and cheap to buy.

Once paunched, remove each leg at the joint with a cleaver, secateurs or a sharp knife. Separate the fur and muscle covering the gut from the skin (it comes away quite easily). Continue to do this until you work your way round to the back of the rabbit. Then pull the skin over the back legs as if taking off a sock; the tail will be dealt with later. Once over the back legs and free, pull the skin forwards and ease over each front leg. The skin (fur) that is left is pulled forwards, exposing the neck. Either skin the head or decapitate it. Remove the tail, anal glands and any remaining organs running through the hips. Once you are happy with the finished article, wipe or wash the carcass and your hands under running water in preparation to joint and cook. Remember that food poisoning is preventable; you should clean your hands and surfaces thoroughly before and after cooking. Avoid contamination, as food poisoning from cooked food often occurs as a result of cross-contamination from raw foods.

OPPOSITE: First you must catch your rabbits. (Greg Knight)

THE AUTHOR'S FAVOURITE RABBIT DISH

Taylor Braised Shoshoi* with Leeks and Cider

Serves four hungry people.

8 prepared ¾ grown rabbit legs

250g pancetta cut into cubes, or lardons of bacon

1 tb sp olive oil

3 tb sp seasoned plain flour

35g butter

3 leeks, washed, trimmed and sliced thinly

500ml Aspall dry cider

284ml carton double cream

1 large sprig fresh thyme

Salt and freshly ground black pepper

Chopped parsley to serve

- Heat the oil in a large pan over a medium heat. Add the pancetta or bacon and cook until browned, take out of the pan, leaving behind the fat, and set aside.

- Toss the rabbit legs in the seasoned flour and fry in the bacon fat until brown all over. This can be done in batches, adding a drop more oil if necessary. Turn off the heat.

- Heat the butter in a separate pan and add the sliced leeks. Cook gently until they are soft and silky.

- Add the leeks to the rabbit legs along with the bacon, cider, cream and thyme sprig. Bring up to a simmer and cook uncovered for one to one and a half hours, stirring occasionally. Cook until the meat is very tender.

- Season to taste with salt and pepper and add chopped parsley. Serve on warm plates with lots of mashed potatoes and buttered green cabbage.

- Serve with a glass of Aspall dry cider and enjoy.

* Shoshoi – old Romany word for rabbit.

Appendix:
Ferreting and the Law

The laws outlined below are designed to be of help to ferreters and those seeking to gain ferreting permission. Familiarity with the requisite legislation will certainly assist those trying to obtain permission to work their ferrets on private land. The laws not only affect what and how we hunt, but also how we treat animals in general, whether it is the rabbit, dog or ferret. Bear in mind that while you are out ferreting or looking to gain new permission, it is the whole of the ferreting community you are representing and not just yourself.

FIREARMS LEGALISATION

All guns used in connection with ferreting must comply with the relevant firearms law and must be held on the relevant firearm or shotgun certificates.

THE GROUND GAME ACT 1880

This gives every occupier of land a limited right to kill and take rabbits and hares concurrently with the right of any other person entitled to do so on the same land. An occupier may use any legal method to kill rabbits, such as gassing, trapping, ferreting, shooting, snaring, netting and, with the exception of shooting, he may authorize other persons to assist him. The Ground Game Act exempts an occupier, and persons authorized by him to kill rabbits, from the need to hold a game licence. There is no close season for rabbits or prohibited time of taking with the exception of the provisions of the Ground Game Act

1880 and 1906, relating to the taking of rabbits on moorland and on unenclosed land.

PROTECTION OF ANIMALS ACT 1911

This Act protects animals against suffering any form of cruelty.

AGRICULTURE ACT 1947

Under section 98 any person having the right to do so may, by written notice, be required by the minister to take such steps as may be necessary for the killing, taking or destruction of certain animals or birds (or their eggs) for the purpose of preventing damage to crops, pasture, animal or human foodstuffs, livestock, trees, hedges, banks or any works of land. The notice may specify time limits for any action, the steps to be taken and the land on which they are to be taken.

Animals that may be specified in the notice are rabbits, hares, other rodents, deer, foxes and moles. There are powers to add other animals to the list. The birds that may be specified are all wild birds not protected by schedule 1 of the Wildlife and Countryside Act 1981. Under section 98(7) (added by Section 2 of the Pest Act 1954) an occupier may be required by written notice to destroy or reduce breeding places or cover (for example, scrub) for rabbits or to prevent rabbits from spreading or doing damage elsewhere.

Under Section 99 occupiers of land may be required to take steps to prevent the escape of animals from land on which they are kept in captivity, but only if the animals are agricultural pests, or animals which might damage banks or land works. Dangerous animals are not included – they are the responsibility of local authorities.

PEST ACT 1954

Rabbit Clearance Orders (under Section1) Rabbit Clearance Order no. 148

This was issued in 1972 and made the whole of England and Wales a rabbit clearance area (excluding the city of London, the isles of Scilly and Skokholm island).

Occupier's Responsibilities in Rabbit Clearance Area (under Section 1)

All occupiers have a continuing obligation to control rabbits living on, or resorting to, their land unless they can establish that it is not reasonably practical for them to do so, when they must prevent the rabbits from doing damage, for example by fencing them in with rabbit-proof fencing. Local authorities have an obligation to control rabbits on their own land.

An occupier within a rabbit clearance area has unrestricted rights to kill rabbits on his land by any lawful means except by shooting.

Spread of Myxomatosis (under Section 12)

It is illegal to use an infected rabbit to spread myxomatosis.

THE ABANDONMENT OF ANIMALS ACT 1960

An Act to prohibit the abandonment of animals, and for purposes connected therewith.

THE 1953 DOGS (PROTECTION OF LIVESTOCK) ACT AND 1970 ANIMALS ACT

These Acts require dogs and ferrets to be kept under control.

WILD MAMMALS (PROTECTION) ACT 1996

Under this Act, it is an offence intentionally to inflict unnecessary suffering, as specified by the Act, on any wild mammal. This legalization may need to be considered where the destruction of occupied warrens and burrow systems is being contemplated. This Act plugs a loophole that existed in wildlife legislation, where non-captive wild animals had little or no protection. It made it an offence to mutilate, kick, beat, impale, stab, burn, crush, drown, drag or asphyxiate any wild animal with intent to cause unnecessary suffering. Exemptions allowed pest control and shooting to be carried out providing that the animal is killed swiftly. This eliminates drowning as a means of dispatching trapped animals.

THE SPECIFIED ANIMAL PATHOGENS ORDER 1998 (S.I.1998/463)

This Order prohibits the introduction into an animal of the live virus causing vital haemorrhagic disease (VHD) of rabbits, except where such introduction is undertaken under the authority of a licence. These prohibitions mean that the deliberate spreading of myxomatosis or VHD cannot be used as a legal method of controlling rabbits.

PROTECTION OF WILD MAMMALS (SCOTLAND) ACT 2002

The following exemption means that it is legal to hunt rabbits with dogs on land where permission has been granted:

Meaning of expressions
In this Act 'wild mammal'.
1 (b) does not include a rabbit.

THE HUNTING ACT 2004

Despite what many non-rabbiting people may think, the Hunting Act 2004 did not ban the use of dogs for hunting rabbits.

Part 1 (Offences) of the Act states:

1 Hunting wild mammals with dogs
A person commits an offence if he hunts a wild mammal with a dog, unless his hunting is exempt.

2 Exempt hunting
(1) Hunting is exempt if it is within a class specified in Schedule 1.

Schedule 1 (Exempt Hunting), section 4 clearly states:

The hunting of rabbits is exempt if it takes place on land:

(a) Which belongs to the hunter, or
(b) Which he has been given permission to use for the purpose by the occupier, or, in the case of unoccupied land, by a person to whom it belongs.

You will note that there is no requirement for permission to be in writing.

S.68 CJPO ACT 1994; S.5 PO ACT 1986; S(1) CRIMINAL DAMAGES ACT 1971; BREACH OF THE PEACE AND COMMON LAW

In England and Wales, where saboteurs trespass upon private land (including water, footpaths, towpaths, bridleways and byways) with the intention of disrupting, obstructing or intimidating, each saboteur commits an offence.

Glossary

Albino An animal with red eyes; the coat is white or creamy in colour.

Bitch Regional term for the female ferret or dog.

Bolt or **bolting** The action of the rabbit when vacating its warren or hiding place in a hurry.

Bolters Ferrets that are reluctant to stay in one place for any amount of time, preferring to bolt and move on.

Buck Male rabbit or a regional word for a male ferret.

Burrow or bury Another name for a warren, of whatever size.

Backed up When a rabbit is tight in a stop end.

Back-netted The action of a rabbit when trying to escape or trying to enter the warren from the outside via a hole that has already got a net set over it.

Bag Either a container in which to carry your equipment or referring to the amount of rabbits caught.

Backfilling Filling in the rabbit's entrance/exit holes after ferreting.

Boltholes These often hidden or overlooked holes are small and designed as an emergency exit for an under-pressure rabbit.

Bottled up A rabbit that is stuck in a stop or dead end.

Boxed in A rabbit that is trapped by a ferret.

Boxes Used for transporting ferrets.

Bramble Blackberry bushes or hedge; rabbits love to make their home in this thorny plant.

Business Collective noun for a group of ferrets.

Chinning A method of dispatching the rabbit by holding the rabbit by the back or shoulder, then placing your palm under the chin and pushing the chin and neck backwards.

Chopping A much disliked, frowned upon and inefficient method of despatching a rabbit. The rabbit is held by its back legs and the person aims a karate-style chop with the side of his flat hand at the rabbit's head/neckline in order to break its neck. The majority of blows are inaccurate, leaving the rabbit injured or unconscious rather than dead, and bruising the meat severely.

Collar Attached to the ferret's neck, usually with a ferret-finder transmitter attached.

Coney Another name for a rabbit.

Dead end The end of a tunnel, either a stop or an unfinished bolt-hole or entrance/exit hole.

Dig/digging If the rabbit does not bolt, it has to be dug out, usually in conjunction with a ferret-finder set.

Dispatching Another word to describe the killing of the rabbit.

Doe Female rabbit or a regional term for female ferret.

Draw cord A length of string around the purse net, which once fixed to the peg, enables the net to work.

Dressing A word used to describe gutting, skinning and portioning a rabbit.

Drummer A slang word for the rabbit, named after its habit of banging its feet (drumming) to alert the others of danger.

Earth A regional name for a rabbit warren.

Electronic ferret finder Essential piece of equipment enabling the ferreter consistently to find the ferret, in order to rescue or retrieve it.

Entrance holes The holes which the rabbit and ferret use to enter the warren.

Exit holes The holes used by the ferret and rabbit to vacate the warren.

Filling in After the rabbit has been dug out, the hole requires filling in, as open holes are not just unsightly but dangerous as well.

Fleas At some time or another fleas will jump from rabbit to ferret to dog or vice versa and are carriers of myxomatosis.

Fleck Piece or scrap of rabbit fur.

Graft An old digging tool or an old word for a spade.

Heat Another way of describing the ferret when it is in season during the spring/summer (on heat).

Hob A male ferret.

Hobble A castrated male ferret.

Hoblet A vasectomized male ferret.

Insect bites A method of transferring a disease such as myxomatosis between rabbits.

Jacket The rabbit's fur.

Jill A female ferret.

Killing/killed under When the ferret has had an opportunity to kill the rabbit underground and has either moved or stuck with the corpse.

Kit A young ferret under the age of sixteen weeks, or your equipment.

Knife Used for gutting and portioning rabbits.

Legging The practice of cutting one hind leg of a rabbit and placing the other through it to make transporting a quantity of rabbits easier.

Leptospirosis A disease found in the urine of rats (also called Weil's disease).

Lie up When a rabbit and ferret are stuck in one spot.

Liner An old method using another ferret to find the location of a stuck ferret.

Litter The name for a collection of baby rabbits or ferrets.

Long net A variety of net used in various lengths to aid ferreting awkward spots.

Lurcher The type of dog commonly used for ferreting.

Myxomatosis A disease affecting rabbits, introduced to the UK in 1953 and present ever since.

Nets Used to catch fleeing rabbits, coming in many forms including purse, poke and long nets.

Oestrus The ferret's season.

Paunching Extracting the guts or intestines from the rabbit.

Pegs Used to fasten the nets to the surrounding ground.

Permission This is vital in order to go ferreting; your ferreting ground is your permission.

Poaching Ferreting without permission.

Poke net A larger double-pegged net similar to the single-pegged purse net.

Polecat The polecat is the animal domesticated to evolve into the ferret. Polecat ferrets are often referred to as polecats.

Pop-hole Another name for a bolt-hole.

Probe A rod with a handle used to probe and test the soil during a dig.

Pug A slang word for a ferret.

Purse net A net used for covering the entrance/exit holes on a warren in order to catch the fleeing rabbit.

Quiet Some call an easily handled ferret 'quiet'; otherwise it is the volume of noise acceptable around a warren.

Receiver The hand-held unit of the ferret finder; it receives the signals from the transmitter collar.

Runs The pathways used by the rabbit.

Scut The rabbit's tail.

Set Another name for a warren.

Shooting Using shotguns to shoot the bolting rabbits.

Skinning Removing the rabbit's fur.

Skulking When a ferret plays about in the entrance to a warren; the ferreter is unable to pick up such an animal.

Spade An essential piece of equipment used to dig out the ferret and rabbit.

Sticker A name to describe a ferret (usually hobs) that will stay with a rabbit for a long time or until dug to.

Stingers Nettles.

Stop end The dead end of a tunnel that the rabbit heads for in order to sit out whatever is hunting the warren.

Thumbing An expression to describe how to extract the urine from the body of a dead rabbit.

Ticks A vector of disease, picked up from the warrens and ferrets' bedding such as straw.

Transmitter An electronic device to aid the location of the ferrets, usually worn around the ferret's neck on a collar.

Unused warren Barren or vacant warren, sometimes serving as a safety sanctuary or a halfway house between home and the feeding area.

Urine The waste fluid of all animals; signals the presence of rabbits in the snow and frost and can carry disease (if from a rat).

VHD Viral haemorrhagic disease.

Warren The home of the rabbit.

Weil's disease A potentially lethal disease also called leptospirosis, found in the urine of rats.

Workers A name given to proven working stock.

Young Juvenile ferrets or rabbits.

Index